THE LOOKING GLASS

Within a Cognitive and Personal Journey

Narrated By

Mark Stone - Sanders

Published by Franklin Publishers

Printed in the United States of America

For permissions, inquiries, or additional copies, contact:

Franklin Publishers

www.franklinpublishers.com

TABLE OF CONTENTS

FOREWORD

⸺⚬⸺

My name is Mark Sanders, but my divine names are Justice Divine Allah, Jihad Damu Askari, and Magnetic Sapient Allah. I am a poor, righteous teacher and an advocate of the Nation of Gods and Earths (NEG), also known as the 5%ers.

I was introduced to this life-saving culture as a young man on 35th and 5th Avenue at Shabazz's Fish and Chips. At the time, it was owned and operated by the Nation of Islam (NOI). In my community, The knowledge I gained remained with me, though it sometimes lay dormant during my descent into savagery.

This work is both a testimony and a cautionary tale—one meant for those who have the wisdom to see beyond the surface, to perceive truth with their mind's eye, their third eye.

The culture I represent was labeled a "Security Threat Group" by state and federal authorities in 1995 despite its origins in righteousness. Founded in 1964 by our educator, Clarence 13X, known as Father Allah, the Nation of Gods and Earths was established as a free cipher—a way of life grounded in divine knowledge. Our culture was even granted tax-exempt status as a 501(c) nonprofit, like other religious organizations, under the First Amendment.

Yet, because we teach that the Black Man is God, the Black Woman is Earth, and the white man is the devil, we are collectively deemed a threat.

The truth, however, is that our culture is all-inclusive. There are white five percenters among us. We are neither pro-Black nor anti-white—we are pro-God and anti-devil. So why are we feared?

Is it because we boldly declare that the Black Man is God and the Black Woman is Earth? No, because when we say these truths, they laugh in our faces. Is it our culture that makes us a threat? No, because 85% of the populace sees our wisdom as something foreign, something that does not fit within their reality.

Perhaps they fear us because we have finally come to understand why we failed in the past—because we now take responsibility for our circumstances rather than blaming others.

Or maybe they fear us because we teach our brothers and sisters behind enemy lines how to free themselves. We advocate for economic self-sufficiency, teaching our people to break the cycle of poverty through education, business development, and community control. By doing this, we give direction and purpose to future generations, leaving them no excuses to choose slavery over freedom.

The Power of Knowledge and Identity

By teaching self-sufficiency, we are giving purpose and direction to the generations that follow. We leave no room for excuses—no justification for choosing slavery over freedom. They began to fear us not because we were anti-white or pro-Black but because we stood against all that is weak and wicked—devilishment. Instead, we uphold righteousness, which is precise, powerful, and produces right conduct.

It is well known that our ancestors along the Nile River educated all of humanity, laying the foundation for civilization itself. Through their knowledge, they civilized the world. What we teach today follows that same mission—it dismantles the falsehood of white supremacy and its origins.

We understand that fear was instilled in our psyche, meant to suppress us. But we have thought deeply, studied extensively, and uncovered the truth through knowledge of self and our ancient ancestors. Through antiquitous Quran (history), we have reached a scientific conclusion: the devil fears us not for who we are but for what we can awaken. He fears our ability to revive the mentally dead, to unite them in righteousness under one common cause.

I know that this culture threatens the power structure of this nation and its so-called justice system. History proves it. Time and again, they have sought to destroy us—wholesale slaughter, bombs dropped on our communities, mass incarceration—all because we stirred the minds of those who had been asleep.

But the real fear is not us as individuals. What they truly fear is the possibility of change. They fear our ability to unite all oppressed people to rise against their oppressor. They fear the power of the unknown becoming known.

Understand this: you are both human and divine, created in His image and likeness. Never lower yourself to be anything less than the God of your own destiny.

In the Nation of Gods and Earths (NEG), we take righteous names to reflect and define our identity—ethnically, morally, and spiritually. Our righteous names affirm our divinity, severing the link to our slave master's name.

While we honor the names given to us at birth, our divine names are bestowed by our educators. These names are based on our character, morality, ethics, and natural order. My own righteous names reflect my attributes:

- **Justice Divine Allah** – Justice represents the penalty or reward for one's actions. Divine is my true self. Allah means God.

- **Jihad Damu Askari** – My Islamic name. Jihad means struggle. Askari is Swahili for soldier.. Damu means blood.

- **Magnetic Sapient Allah** – Magnetic signifies my ability to attract. Sapient means wise and discerning. And Allah, once again, means God.

Each of these names is a reflection of my reality. They are not just words but representations of my purpose, my being, and my divinity.

Along with mastering 120 degrees of knowledge to be born again, I also had to understand everything in existence through the expressions of signs, symbols, numbers, and letters. As I stated, in English, Allah means God. Allah is He who knows, understands, and controls the elemental forces—strong, electromagnetic, weak, and gravitational. He also governs the five fundamental energies: chemical, electrical, mechanical, nuclear, and thermal—each existing within the self, each proving the motion of life.

All praise is due to Allah, Lord of all the worlds.

Supreme peace and blessings.

Before we begin this journey, I want to share five words of wisdom—principles to live by every day:

1. Life is beautiful.

2. Strive to train harder.

3. Be honest with yourself.

4. Express yourself 100%.

5. Respect yourself and others.

For over 2,000 years, our enemy has understood the power of words and has used them against us—to keep us divided, blind, and sleepwalking, incapable of seeing the lies we are fed daily through the media.

The Honorable Louis Farrakhan once spoke on the power of words. He explained how the word "Negro" was limited and how the Honorable Elijah Muhammad used the term "Black" in a way that connected us to our people worldwide. This connection ran deep—so much so that when Patrice Lumumba was assassinated in the Congo, Black people in America demonstrated at the United Nations. When Martin Luther King Jr. was murdered, over a hundred cities were set on fire. The language Elijah Muhammad used created a nervous system within us, allowing us to feel each other's pain no matter where we were.

Seeing this, the enemy intensified their study of us. They wanted to understand who or what had the power to ignite an entire people into action. They discovered that it wasn't just a single leader—it was the way language was used. The media had given us a shared attitude toward white people and the establishment, an attitude that solidified into a collective belief.

We shared a common understanding of the police, the government, and white supremacy—one that was deeply real. This belief grew into an ideology, and that ideology bound us together as a national community despite our differences in groups, churches, and mosques.

When the enemy saw that television had served this purpose—when the names "Black," "brother," and "sister" had caused us to see ourselves as kin to people of color all over the world—they knew they had to change the language.

They started by reintroducing the term "minority." And once we accepted it, we accepted the frame of mind that came with it. The truth—that we are a majority—was erased.

We became "disadvantaged."

We became "African Americans."

But what happened to us as a result of accepting that language? It killed the nervous system that the language of Blackness had created.

Then, every television show that once had "Black" in its name as an adjective was changed. "Black News" in New York, "Black Journal," "Black Star Program" in Baltimore—every city had something Black to describe the main noun. Then, "Black Journal" became "Tony's Journal," and "Black News" was eventually taken off the air.

"Black Star" was gone.

Now, you have programs on television with the term "Black" in front of it, but their purpose is no longer the same.

The enemy understood the value of language. They knew that if you shift the language, you shift perception.

What they did was kill the nervous system that once connected us as a family. Then we could become tribes—divided—and kill one another without feeling the pain of our brothers in the Caribbean, in Brazil, or in Africa. We became less and less global—our focus narrowed until it was reduced to gangs, religious denominations, and organizations. We killed each other throughout America and never really felt the pain.

We are one family united by holy blood.

Our lives do matter, and we are under attack by the same enemy.

Don't be fooled—look at this fool Trump. The enemy is still the enemy. We are still targeted for murder.

We are still trapped in a threefold system of genocide by the powers that be:

1. Healthcare.

2. The criminal (in)justice system.

3. Law enforcement's targeted killings of Black men and women.

I hope that you enjoy and digest what I have to communicate to you. Understand that I wrote this in my cell—not to glorify the so-called game but to show you that the game is set up for us to lose. The game never loves you back.

A lifestyle that does not advocate life—a positive, productive life—is not a lifestyle. It is a deathstyle. And it leads to the second door of no return for Black and Brown people—prison. The new slave plantation. The new slave market. They buy and sell us on Wall Street now. Private prison stock. We are once again property. Cheap slave labor. Keeping us asleep and incarcerated is a billion-dollar industry.

Open your eyes. See what you are looking at—don't just look at what you see. I hope my words of wisdom open your eyes to the truth, to the lies being told. Find a teacher. Be a teacher to a young person. Bulletproof love and solidarity. Struggle until we win—or at least don't lose.

Officer Bernard Bennett (1946-1970) was critically wounded by a sniper's bullet from a rooftop as he drove his patrol car through an Oak Park neighborhood on May 9, 1970. The bullet ripped through the roof of the car and struck Officer Bennett in the back of the head. His partner, Officer Lloyd Smothers, was unharmed. Bennett, a Viet- nam veteran on the force two years, died on May 13, 1970. This attack occurred during heightened tensions be- tween the police and the African American community in the Oak Park area. Two members of the Black Panther Party, Jack Strivers and Mark Teemer, and two nonmem- bers, Booker Cooke and Ceriaco Cabrallis, later known as the Oak Park Four, were arrested for the killing. The men were ultimately acquitted due to lack of evidence, the case remains unsolved.

P.E.A.C.E.

INTRO

I came up at a time and in an environment where the game—a game that is not a game in reality—is glamorized by the media and sold to our babies as something to participate in. But in truth, the game is not a game. Lives are lost. Lives are damaged beyond repair.

This so-called game will destroy you. It is designed for you to lose—to play for a hot second before being captured by the powers that be, left to sit down and count too many calendars.

I invite you to take a short mind trip with me—to my home, the streets that trained me, honed my skills as an apex predator, and shaped my view of reality from a tender age.

In closing, I want the reader to know:

No matter how much you love it, this game will never love you back.

She is a trifling, dirty b*tch—loyal to no one. She gives you short intervals of pleasure and long-running periods of pain, tragedy, and confusion.

Pick your poison.

Get in and get out.

—M.S.

CHAPTER ONE

I was bred and raised in the capital of California—Sacramento, to be exact, a.k.a. Sac Town, Mackamento. The Oak Park community is my native home—Sac's first suburb, the oldest Black community in the city, and one of the largest. It also carries the title The Murder Midz. Our population exceeds 50,000 residents, give or take, maybe more.

Those of my generation were essentially the offspring of the Black Power movement, primarily the Black Panther Party for Self-Defense. As a consequence, we had a rudimentary esprit de corps of Black power and unity. We were the survivors of the war waged against Black activist groups in the late 1960s and early '70s—targeted by the government and law enforcement operations like COINTELPRO under the direction of FBI Chief J. Edgar Hoover.

The essence of that war still lingered in my hood in the early '80s. But I digress—allow me to bring you home with me. Sacramento, California—the state capital—sits 70 miles west of the San Francisco Bay Area.

The Black Panthers were located in the heart of Oak Park in the 1960s. The BPP gained national attention in 1967—the year I was born, the Yin-Yang year, also known as the Equality God year.

1967 was the year the Black Panthers marched on the California State Capitol, walking onto the lawmakers' floors where the state's laws were enacted. Ronald Wilson Reagan was governor at the time, and the Panthers scared the hell out of the white folks up there. Some even had to rent suits to get assemblyman Willie Brown, who was the only Black state lawmaker at the time, to speak on their behalf.

The Sacramento chapter of the BPP was located in Oak Park, with Brother Charles Bronson serving as captain. Their office was at **2981 35th Street**, right off 5th Avenue. On this same street stood Oak Park's first street organization—the first street tribe in Sacramento—called the Black Souls. Next to them was the NOI (Nation of Islam), which owned and operated a fish and chips joint called Shabazz's Fish & Chips. This corridor along 35th Street and 5th Avenue was thriving.

Back then, this area was like Oak Park's downtown, packed with nightclubs, stores, and businesses. Gambling shacks, liquor stores, and Joe's Style Shop—which sold the latest fashions, tailored suits, and hats—lined the street. The flyest clothes of the era could be found here. It was cracking all along 35th Street on the 5th.

At this time in Sacramento's history, if you were a person of color, you faced discrimination at every level of the establishment. Outright racism was rampant, and no love or mercy was shown. The police would kill you just as they do now if you were Black or Brown. Finding housing was extremely difficult, and very few Africans lived downtown. Schools were still segregated, and Black people were redlined into specific neighborhoods. Banks and real estate agents refused to sell homes to Black and Brown families in predominantly white areas. It wasn't until a lawsuit was brought against the city in the 1970s that Black families were allowed to buy homes outside of Oak Park, Del Paso Heights, and Rancho Cordova.

Sacramento, at the time, had two major Air Force bases—Mather and McClellan. My father worked at McClellan for over 20 years. The town was a place where ex-cops and military types came to retire. Sacramento,

California—a city full of redneck crackers—had police brutality at its highest point in the 1960s.

During this time, the city's population exceeded 67,000. Black people were regularly harassed just for being in Sacramento's largest park, William Land Park, which was less than two miles from Oak Park. The dividing line was Highway 99, built in 1962. It literally split the white side from the Black side—some deep South Jim Crow shit right here in California.

Black people were only allowed to congregate and patronize McClatchy Park—the Big Park—located at 33rd Street on 5th Avenue.

CHAPTER TWO

———⚬———

L ocated just one block from the Black Panther office, the Big Park, as we affectionately called it, was home to a growing BPP chapter. Membership quickly expanded, with brother-and-sister teams like James Mott, Gloria Abernathy, Mark Teemer, Margo Rose, Melvin Whitaker, Eugene Boaltle, Links Haskins, Jeff Howe (a.k.a. Time Bomb), Delores Henderson, Jack Strivers, and many more courageous brothers and sisters who were committed to saving themselves and their community. They fed the babies free breakfast.

Mark Teemer, a Vietnam veteran, sketched the Black Panther coloring book. All these righteous Black folk worked to uplift and liberate our community, defending it against the murderous and racist actions of law enforcement during this era. They volunteered their time to support the many social programs being implemented.

To become a Panther during this time of reconstructing our minds and rebuilding our community, one had to be vetted and go through a rigorous six-week reeducation program. This training included studying political and military science, all led by the chapter's information officer. The Panther Paper was sold, political reeducation was taught, and self-defense—both personal and for the community—was encouraged in response to the hostile and dangerous climate of the time.

4

The street organization The Black Souls had a clubhouse on 35th Street. One of my big homies, Junie Darden (a.k.a. Frame), was a member, a mentor, and my first baseball coach.

JoJo Waters, Coop, Donnie Pitts, and a few more of my big homies were also under The Black Soul thang—and they were about handling business.

They patrolled the park, watched over the hood, mentored the youth, and ran an anti-poverty program. They understood that this was—and still is—the inner city, the ghetto. In fact, The Black Souls were even granted government funding for their anti-poverty program in the late '60s. But the cat who got the money ran off with it—never spending a dime on the people who actually needed it.

At the time, President Richard Nixon—or Tricky Dick, a first-class war criminal and avowed racist—was in office. He was handing out all kinds of grants, not because he cared, but because Black people were waking up to the truth about this nation.

The masses were rising up, and cities were burning. The devil was scared. So they did what they always do—gave us just enough to pacify us and lull us back to sleep. And eventually, they succeeded. The boys in my hood were getting money. We had always been hittas and go gettas.

At the same time, The Nation of Islam was also a very dynamic force in Oak Park.

All Black nationalist groups of that time owed their beginnings to the life-giving, self-saving ideology of the Honorable Elijah Muhammad. It was at Shabazz's Fish & Chips that I was first told that the Black man is God by nature. My big homies—Jabbar, Big Winfred, and John Usher—dropped that knowledge on me around 1973.

I was six or seven years old when I first learned the truth about who the Black man really is—that we were first, the original man and God by nature. That knowledge had a profound effect on me.

At that time, my road dog was Kevin "Flashlight" Cheney—my relative, my lifelong loyal comrade. May he rest in peace. I miss him dearly—he was more like a brother than a friend. We did everything together, and he was lucky enough to avoid the penitentiary.

While the BPP was thriving in my community and nationwide, a conspiracy was unfolding at the state and federal levels. The powers that be were outright murdering Panthers—and, in general, killing any Black people who stood up for themselves and demanded their God-given right to be human.

The police tear-gassed the Panther office in Oak Park—and they hit The Black Souls, too.

In this oppressive environment, a pig's life was cut short one early morning in Oak Park on 35th Street. Four Panthers were arrested. This would become known as the Oak Park 4 case. The charges? Trumped-up. Fabricated.

Before the incident, the BPP had declared martial law in Oak Park. The year was 1969, and the Panthers issued a warning—petty grievances would **not** be tolerated on 35th Street. They refused to let disunity tear the community apart.

CHAPTER THREE

The BPP had sent out a notice to sponsoring groups that there would be no more personal hang-ups or petty squabbles—there were bigger things going on at the time.

In 1970, when a police officer got his dome knocked off on 35th Street by sniper fire, the city responded with immediate retaliation. As I mentioned before, this led to the Oak Park 4 case, which was eventually beaten due to lack of evidence. After the case was dismissed, the city came out to Oak Park and started cutting down trees along 35th Street and in the Big Park, claiming that Panthers were using them as cover to shoot at police. The irony is Oak Park got its name because of those very oak trees.

The federal government had already been playing dirty. They sent fake letters about Panther members, accusing them of being informants or snitches, sowing doubt and division within the ranks. This was part of the COINTELPRO, the Counterintelligence Program—a government operation designed to prevent the rise of a so-called Black Messiah. The goal was simple: divide and conquer. It was the same Willie Lynch mentality, pitting us against each other for their benefit and our destruction.

The Majestics car club was on 33rd Street—these cats were about that life, too.

The Panther office was right next to the post office, which is still standing on 35th Street today. It remains one of the oldest post offices in the city, a historical landmark. But by then, the era of Black Power was coming to an end, not just in Sacramento but across the nation. They were slaughtering our people wholesale—coast to coast. A new era was creeping in, one that would have devastating consequences for New African communities everywhere. But this wasn't something new; it had been lurking in the shadows for years, hiding in the deep recesses of the community. Now, it would rear its ugly head, and the whole hood would take notice. The devastation would last until the next wave of societal destruction hit—and when it did, my generation would feel it firsthand.

Now here we were, coming of age, looking at this vibrant, live-ass place we called home. And shit was bracking—never a dull moment. Not one.

It had everything under the sun and under the moon—every vice you could think of and then some. Drugs, sex, violence—you name it.

We had three high schools in the community: Sacramento High, Christian Brothers High (a private school), and American Legion High (a continuation school). I attended both Sac High and American Legion. Depending on where you lived, you could also attend CK McClatchy or Hiram Johnson. There was even a fourth high school on Sacramento Boulevard, now MLK Boulevard, called Leland Stanford High School— but two of my older homies burned it down in the late '60s. Today, the Oak Park Community Center and Father Keith B. Kinney Elementary sit where it once stood.

So here we were, deep in the 1970s. And just like in the mid-to-late '60s, heroin was king in the neighborhood. That James Brown song King Heroin? Yeah, it was knocking.

Heroin was a plague in most inner cities at the time, and mine was no exception. But it wasn't just dope—other extracurricular activities were cracking, too. Pimping, pandering, boosting, gambling—it was all going down, day and night, and extra heavy on Sundays.

CHAPTER FOUR

At this time, I'm living on 36th Street—3516, 36th Street to be exact—between 12th Avenue, 10th Avenue, and 9th Avenue, right between Silo Baptist Church and Trinity Baptist Church. I'm running behind my brothers: Little James Reed (52 Reed for Sac High football team), Big James, Jerome, and my relatives Detchie, Vince (a.k.a. Hot Zilla), and Darrell Smith.

I looked up to all my uncles who had been to prison—from the 1950s and '60s all the way to the '80s. My relative John Earl, my aunt Eddie May's son from Orange, Texas, had come to California from Orange and was a maniac—a stone-cold, stomp-down killer. Gangsta and some mo' shit. All of my extended family had been under some form of community control by the powers that be—juvenile hall, the boys' ranch, all of that shit we, as people of color, encounter and endure here in the wilderness of North America. Only my uncle Johnny and my dad's brother Harold had avoided prison's indignities. This was my introduction to life as I saw it, and to me, it was normal. The prison was normal. Violence was normal.

I went to Bret Harte Elementary School with niggas who were destined to be major players in this game that is not a game. Fat Kev (a.k.a. Kevin Hooks), Kirk Crump, Kenny Pitts, Chris Hobson, Donald

Hair—whose father was a teacher at our school and a strong Black man—Jeff Bally, Marvin Seward, Shawn Powells, Anthony Cannon, Bruce and Ken Johnson, Stacy Goodson, Demetrious Jones, Willie (One Five) Hill, Fat Bobo. A gang of us. We ran hard. Did our thang. Had fun in a very violent, poverty-stricken environment.

We used to kick used needles in the alleys—the fiends would leave them all over the ground. My second-to-oldest uncle, Clarence, was about that life in the '50s, '60s, and '70s. I remember my mother taking me to visit him in San Quentin in the early '70s—he had shot a police officer in Frisco. All of my uncles—Jimmy, Puddin, J.T., J.B.—and my relative John Earl had all been sent to California's penal colonies starting in the early '50s. Up until the '80s, John Earl was in Soledad with George Jackson during the very turbulent '60s.

I was never aware that the environment I lived in was violent. Shit, as a young child, my doctor used to make house calls to check up on me and my sister Felicia. Dr. Morrissy had an office on 40th Street and 11th Avenue. Back in the day, growing up in the hood, we all had the same doctor—most of us had even been delivered by the same doctor. Because of the racist-ass practices in Sacramento at the time, Dr. Morrissy had a thriving medical practice. White folks didn't want nothing to do with us.

The segregation they were enforcing was illegal, but as always, when the devil makes the laws, it will never be fair. Until lions have historians, the tale of the hunt will always glorify the hunter. The laws were against us then, and they're still against us now, 50+ years later.

Like I was saying, where I lived was dangerous, but as a child, it was just what I knew. I ran with a pack of wild niggas. We stayed in shit or started some shit. I stayed fighting—was tall for my age.

The biggest park in my community was The Big Park, also called The Park, on 33rd and 35th Avenue. A huge park with two baseball diamonds, two basketball courts, an Olympic-style pool, a kid's pool, a playground, and massive oak trees. Those oak trees gave plenty of shade during the long, hot summers. The Big Park—it was like baby Africa, the Serengeti.

Before they built the "New Pool" in '80/81, I learned to swim in the old pool, which had a depth of seven and a half feet and a slide. There was no diving board, and the water was ice cold in the summer months. This was the epicenter of the community—still is in some ways—but back then, it really was the heart of Oak Park. We spent all summer at this park. It was the unofficial babysitter of the community.

There was a time when you could leave your kids anywhere in the neighborhood, and they'd be safe, sound, and in good hands. It truly was a village back then. Anyone's mother or father had permission to get dat ass if you were fucking up.

Not like nowadays. Times change. Cycles repeat.

"Nobody frees a slave; a slave must free himself."

- Marcus Garvey

As I was saying before, heroin was king at this time. Niggas were getting turned out on that thang. I was still in preschool. My uncle Puddin was going with Granny—Helen Hawkins, matriarch of the Mad Pad.

Back then, the Mad Pad was off 43rd and Broadway. Broadway separates North Oak Park from South Oak Park. There are two ZIP codes in the community—95817 and 95820. That's where I'd get babysat while my mother worked during the day. Lala would watch me—really, the whole Hawkins family did.

My big homie, Roland Hawkins, Granny's son, had a twin sister named Rosie, but Roland was having his cash back then. In the early '70s, he was making bread selling them Red Devils—the ecstasy of that era. Barbiturates. They sold like hotcakes in the hood. Selling pussy was like shaking hands, and macking was like breathing. My niggas ain't have no options but to get it and be about it!

It was in the air—contagious. Everybody was trappin', robbin', stealin', and killin'! I saw my first homicide up close and personal in 1975, right around the corner from the house I grew up in. Live and in color. And it ain't like the movies. I saw my second murder by firearm a block over across 12th Ave. a while later. One of my older homies killed another over a pit bull fight.

This was common in my region. Not as common as the hype would later devolve into, but still a part of life.

Violence was the undercurrent of every street back then. Marvin Drayton was killed that same year. Dante Drayton was stabbed to death the next year, 1976, up at Mr. Dee's nightclub on Stockton Boulevard.

I was growing up fast, seeing things a child shouldn't see. But the hood does that to you. You realize early that only the strong survive and thrive. And sometimes, your strength makes a weaker individual kill you out of cowardice.

I was trying to emulate the men in my family—trying to dress like them move like them. They were my role models. My relatives Detchie, Hot, my brothers Lil' James, Big James, and Jerome, and my relly Darrell Smith—who was a muthafuckin' player and a mack—would all become major influences in my life.

Time was flying, and the game was advancing. During this period, there were three major dope tracks in the hood—on fire. Open-air shit. This was also the gold weed era. The early '70s, niggas was getting rich.

My big homies were major players—boss players and bosses. Niggas like Big Rudy, Lee Cross, and John Powells. I remember Big Rudy bought a Rolls-Royce off the lot—brand new. Lee Cross was pushing a phat-ass Harley-Davidson chopper, some real Easy Rider shit.

Donnie Pitts was cross-country pimping, so was Robert Crump (Knock-Knock), D.W., Melvin Walker, Blue Felix, Quack, Ronnie Bean, Shaver Ellis, and Bo Slauson.

And you had stomp-down gangstas like Ray Dick, Leon Murphy, Levall Murphy, and Dennis Miller. All these cats were about that life.

CHAPTER FIVE

There was a gambling shack on Stockton Boulevard at Springer's Liquor Store, right off Broadway. A gas station sat nearby. This was right at the corner of Stockton Boulevard and Broadway. Across the street from Springer's was the Joy Riders car club.

An older brother who lived up the street from me on 9th Avenue and 36th was someone I used to soak up game from on a regular basis—a solid dude, a teacher, a big homie to me. We called him Cousin Sam. He was the first millionaire in my hood that I knew of who got it out the game.

When I knew him as a young boy, he was already past the point of just being a "rich nigga." He was very low-key, under the radar, but he had one of the phattest houses in the hood—probably still does. I remember watching him have a Black man carved into a statue out of an old oak tree that had been struck by lightning. Instead of letting the tree go to waste, he turned it into a work of art. I sat there and watched as a sculptor—someone he paid—carved the image of a strong Black man out of that tree.

Cousin Sam would be killed sometime later at the gambling shack, trying to break up a fight between two of his friends.

Around this time, I was taking martial arts lessons up at the old **U.S. Bank** building on Broadway—Broadway and 35th Street, to be exact. They taught us kung fu, Chinese kickboxing, and boxing, and there were weights in the basement of the center. This was a temporary community center until the new one was built almost ten years later at MLK Boulevard and 9th Avenue.

There was a huge martial arts scene in the early '70s. Bruce Lee flicks were all the rage, along with the Blaxploitation films of the era. A gang of us were up in there getting trained and learning the arts. Myself Shy, his older brother Bobo (Bo Slim), and my bros' relatives were all taking part in the program offered by the brothers teaching at the center.

So learning and growing was going on.

A quick retrospective view.

The ability to see shows a person the way.

- Kikuyu-Proverb

So, I guess the logical question is—why did I, along with many of my peers, fall into crime? Why did we develop a disregard not only for the legitimacy of the so-called Amerikkkan government but also for its socioeconomic structures and the politics of a nation supposedly founded on a constitution that recognized all its citizens as equals? A nation that later instituted amendments to that same constitution, supposedly guaranteeing equal protections, especially for citizens of color?

Well, as an adolescent child of African/Asiatic descent, I possessed—along with many children of color—a socially intuitive duality. The tranquil comforts of love and the anxiety of hate. The companionship of acceptance and the insecurity of rejection.

Unfortunately, as I grew older and came into contact with the dominant social structure and institutions of this society, my intuition became more defined, while the balance of my experiences became lopsided. My character was no longer shaped solely by my own choices— it was being defined by the color of my skin.

15

For those of you who understand this, you know how it can become a powerful motivating factor in the decisions we make as a whole—a nation of marginalized people of color. Too often, it pushes us toward the threshold of the prison door—the door of no return.

I have to bounce back to the place I left you—so be patient and take this trip with me.

CHAPTER SIX

Emergence of game

As I was coming into my adolescence, I was growing up in the era of Blaxploitation. Becoming a man-child. At just 10 or 11 years old, I was already pushing six feet tall—gangly, smoking big weed, puffing Newport menthols, and drinking Old English malt liquor. Trying to be like the older males in my immediate family who, at the time, were my examples of manhood.

My big relatives—Detchie, Darrel, Hot, my brothers Lil' James, Big James, and Jerome—along with my many uncles and older homies shaped how I saw the world. Cats like Doug Wayne, Base Pipe Mike, Walter Anderson, Chp Pitts, Donnie Pitts, Tony Ellis, Leon Murphy, Carl Murphy, Levall Murphy, James Usher, Pete Brown, Wayne Moses, Leroy Craig, Big Virgil, Shawn Collins, Randy Moses, and Roland Hawkins—just to name a few.

At this time, I was running the streets hard with Bunny (Cleveland Jackson), Derek Brown (Mr. Fix), Clemmie Bad Mouth Fields, Ronnie Fields (a.k.a. Peg Leg), Leon Jordan, Marvin Seward, my relative Carl

Webb, Shy (Chi) Francci Noel and his brother Bobo, and Stephen Miles. We'd be up in the Big Park with Frankalane, Leroy Woods, and Kenny Pitts—just way too many cats to name right now. Jeff Baily lived across the street from me at this time, too.

I spent my days hanging out at the Mad Pad on 37th, right around the corner from my house and next door to Cathy and Cindy Redman's joint. I was also up on 7th Avenue—a.k.a. Wall Street—with my relly Hot, Duncan Hawkins, and Big Q. Walter Anderson was at Stan's joint—Stan the Man, a.k.a. Stanley Prince—along with Reggie, Tim, and Clint Givens' brother.

We called 7th Avenue Wall Street because of the money that flowed through that spot every single day back in the early 1970s. Huge amounts of cash moved through that one street by the hour. They could easily push a couple of pounds in just a few hours on that track back then.

Nixon was president, and the weed was gold weed—strong, pungent marijuana. The same weed Nixon had sprayed with paraquat in Mexico for his so-called war on drugs. A war that's still being faked today.

I'd venture to say that three or four pounds of weed were knocked off daily on that block. Just in the go-backs, there'd be plastic trash cans full of nickel bags posted up on the porch, with about three more in the driveway on the side of the front porch at Stan's spot. My big homies, Chp Pitts and Randy Moses, were always out there. The work would be sacked up across the street, upstairs in Reggie Prince's joint. Stan's brother Clint—the oldest—was the only one about gunplay.

That street was rollin' all day. Big paper collecting.

Shop shut down abruptly at 11 PM each night. Cars lined up bumper-to-bumper on that block, everyone coming through to cop that good gold weed. Fools would get off work from their state and county jobs and slide through Wall Street to pick up a sack before heading home to relax.

We'd be posted up thick as thieves, music knocking, having a good old ghetto life time.

Joe Davis had the alley on 5th Avenue cracking—right off Broadway. Big weed was also being pushed out that alley, right in the back of Thompson's Funeral Home.

The spot on 5th Avenue was just as live—drive-through service. You didn't even have to get out of your car. Just roll through the alley, get served, and be on your way in seconds. The sacks were fat. The alley on 5th shielded you from the prying eyes of the street, so no one could see the transactions going down. You'd drive straight through, hit Broadway, and keep it moving.

Joe Davis had two brothers, Frank and Paul Davis (a.k.a. Shitty), and a nephew named Stretch. Frank Davis used to run hard with my brother Jerome when I was a young blood. I used to post up on 5th Avenue with Stretch, Andre Washington, and Tyrone Jackson, too. P Funk had the water—PCP—cracking, and so did the Barons off of 3rd Avenue. That hop—that thang was being pushed heavy at the Big Park and Sweets Pool Hall on Sacramento Boulevard, which is now MLK Boulevard.

Springer's on Broadway was another hot spot for that hop traffic. The back of the liquor store had an area called The Log—and just like all these other spots, it was doing it to death, day in and day out. This was everyday life in my community at the time. The atmosphere was electric. The hood was jumping.

Niggas were robbing banks. There were whole cliques of robbery crews. The Wild Bunch was knocking down banks—quick, in and out, snatching paper. My big homie, Gangsta Pete, was a professional bank robber. Pete was a master of that takeover-style bank robbery. And when you get caught and prosecuted for that kind of heist? It always goes federal. But the biggest thing going on was pimping and hoeing.

Niggas was low-riding—P Funk, Jackie Blair, Cadillac Jack, Fat Mack—all of them had clean-ass lowriders. Hydraulics were crackin'.

The rims? Either Supremes or Cragars. Moons were popular, too. 520 tires on 13s or 14s. This was way before True Classics and True Spoke wire rims came out.

My relatives were deep in it—Detchie, Darrel Smith, and his brothers Kenny and Vernon, a.k.a. Boo. We used to call BooBerry. He was one of my favorite relatives to run with—we were the same age. Ol' pimpin'-ass Vernon Smith.

Around this time, my big relative Detchie was running around the city, bustin' his gun, turning out house parties, and knocking niggas out that weren't from the hood. Anywhere we went.

Back then, there were only two real ghettos in Sacramento—Oak Park and DPH, Del Paso Heights—or, as we called it, the Deepest Part of Hell.

South Sacramento and other areas? They were nice communities at this time in the city's history. The Elders, a.k.a. Glenn Elder, was also a Black hood back then, but it wasn't as gritty as The P and DPH. The Black scholar Dr. Cornel West is from Glenn Elder—he even went to church in Oak Park at shilo Baptist Church as a child.

But at this time, the only two hoods that really had it poppin' were DPH and Oak Park—at least as far as the underworld was concerned. Period.

The rest of the city? Square bear shit. There were no drug spots or dope tracks in any other part of the city except for DPH and Oak Park. That's why people from all over Sacramento flocked to these two communities in the late '60s and early '70s to fulfill their vices. Whether it was weed, coke, speed, heroin, or gambling—you could get it all in Oak Park or Del Paso Heights.

And back then, all the lil' fast, tall b*tches from the South area? They wanted to fuck with a P nigga. I remember that time with lucidity. Niggas were getting paper. I was hanging with real G's—Charlie Bonton, Leander Cook—up at the Big Park.

Roland Hawkins had a weed spot on 33rd, right by the alley—pumping big weed out that thang. Me and Mert—Lala's oldest son, Roland's sister, and family to me as well—were up in Roland's joint daily, smoking big weed.

The big economies—Leo and John Powels, my neighbor SP's father—they were all getting it in. Big Spooner and Loner were supplying the whole hood with pounds of that good gold weed.

The whole stroll—the track—was on 4th and T Street back then, right around Southside Park. It was a fast track for a city the size of Sac. A gang of state employees would patronize that track. Lots of white tricks were buying pussy by the pound down there.

Traffic would be bumper-to-bumper, day and night. That track had the city buzzing, but it also brought public outcry—shit was even on the news. The problem? It was too close to the park, too close to a couple of schools, and too close to the State Capitol. A couple of my homegirls were even killed on that track.

This was a fast track. Niggas from my hood and the Heights were getting hoe money off of it. We used to ride our bikes down there and fuck with the hoes all the time—me, P. Baby, Stephen Miles, and a few other homies.

Just kids, but trying to see if we could knock a hoe off—or at least get a couple dollars for trying.

We were hoe harassers—just lil' pests to the hoes, trying to get their trap right for the day or night to pay a pimp. 4th and T was doing it—live and in color—especially at night. And we all know—the freaks come out at night. That applied to both the tricks and the hoes.

They did big business under the cover of darkness. At night, the tricks would line up like a drive-through fast food joint, and the hoes would holler for a dollar or duck for a buck. Jumping in and out of cars.

Motels were right around the corner. Plus, fools had rooms in the old Victorian homes down there. Bottom line—the tricks were plentiful, the hoes were getting money, and the pimps were getting that paper socked to their pocket—hard and fast.

My older homies Knock-Knock (Robert Crump), D.W. (Darrel Williams), Donnie Pitts, and Tree Top were pimpin' cross-country— from Hawaii to L.A., from the Big Apple to the Pineapple.

These niggas would pop back in town from trappin'—flossin' them Lacs and Lincolns. They were out there foxin', gettin' it with the crooks. They were crookin', and the hoes were hookin'. These niggas were playing the game that is not a game—playing and scoring.

Sinning and winning. Major players. Major macks. Doing what niggas in my hood were bred and born to do. And in the Heights? There were major macks, too—pimpin'-ass Rico, Joe Fair, Ike Ray, and a few more.

CHAPTER SEVEN

My older homie Blue Felix was getting it too, having his paper dragged up out a hoe's ass. He was a rare combination—Playa and Gangsta. Really, three types of nigga in one. Mack, playa, and gangsta. Not to be played with about his paper or his gangsta.

He was a notorious gorilla pimp, but he had finesse, too—he was also a cross-country pimp. His father, Rich Jimmy, was a major player and a head-splitter. A real live mack and a gangsta, really about that life.

When I was a young child, Rich Jimmy ran an after-hours joint and a gambling spot. It stayed open seven days a week in the hood. As a young blood, I went through there a few times with my pops and uncles. It wasn't uncommon to see kids in these spots—most of the kids lived there.

Blue had two brothers and a sister—Dennis Miller and Johnny Felix. The only girl was Janice Felix. They were all in the game, fully participating.

I was also running tough with my relative Carl Webb and the homie Shawn Duncan (S.D.), who came from a large family—Poo Duncan, Peter Duncan, Darren Duncan, Connie Duncan, and Toni Duncan. One of the biggest families in Oak Park.

S.D. was my bro. He's resting now. I miss my bro—he was my dog at this time.

Poo, whom we called Man back then, was holding it down on Wall Street, acting as Stan's lieutenant, running his machine over on 8th Avenue and getting paid.

Stan, at the time, had a clean-ass Cadillac Brougham (Ham Sandwich), candy red. Eventually, he put star wires and Vogue tires on it, plus a TV in the back. Star wires had just come out—they may have been Cadillac wire rims. This was back in the '70s, though. He was riding clean—Board of Health clean.

The older homie L.K. was living across the street from the neighborhood park, a.k.a. 4th Avenue Park, as it's known now. Hippy was also there—Mrs. Usher's son, my homie Conrad's uncle, and one of my real dogs.

Conrad would become my road dog for a good minute. We hustled together, got on shit together, and raised all kinds of hell together as young bloods. He would be one of my first peers to become a victim of gun violence—one of many. He was murdered in 1982 over some bullshit.

The first was Marvin Keola, who was only 14 when he was killed by a Middle Eastern cat.

This was around 1978. The dude had just migrated to the United States from Iran during that whole exodus when the region was in turmoil because of the Shah and his corrupt dealings with that old snake, the USA.

Marvin was shot 22 times while hiding under the bed of Nora Yaya. The son, Abdul Yaya, took the case, and the family hired a prominent Black attorney to defend him. But the fix was in.

The outcome was evident, just like it is now. Back then, just as today, Black life had little value. A slap on the wrist was all that was given to the perpetrators of the crime.

Anyway, this was the community back then—bumpin' and grindin', live and crackin'. Never a dull moment. I was, needless to say, enjoying my adolescence.

There was always a dice game at the Big Park, every day, in broad daylight. I'd ride my bike up there and shoot dice with my Uncle Jimmy, who was fresh out the pen—for about the second or third time. Unc would let me hit his bottle, shoot dice, and smoke one or two of his Pall Mall cigarettes.

As I said before, the hood was changing. It was so violent at this time that they had begun to call Oak Park Dodge City. You'd have to be at least 50 years old or older to remember this time in Oak Park's history. Fools stayed getting shot.

This was just a few years before my father passed away—from what usually kills Black men too young. Heart disease and high blood pressure.

My father died of a heart attack. I vividly remember those times, as one does their wonder years. Pops would take me and my sister down to L.A.—Compton, to be exact—to visit Aunt Maggie, his sister, who lived on Cherry Avenue in Fruit Town Piru Hood.

My eldest uncle, Johnny, had a daughter in West L.A., too, and I'd visit her with my mother whenever we went down to L.A. Cecilia was her name. I'd kick it with my folks every time Pops took us down there.

Shit was changing fast. I was growing up—growing up fast. Fucking with fast-ass girls running around with them hot pants on. You'd have to have some age on you to remember them hot pants. I was chasing young tramps, and they were chasing me back.

There was this thing my older relatives used to do to me, my relative Kevin Chaney and Boo. If we weren't actively trying to knock a young b*tch, they'd be merciless with the teasing. Calling us B*tchBoy and Pussy Mouth. That alone made us try to get as many girls as possible.

We were actively pursuing two things—paper and pussy. In that order. Purse first, ass last. And these niggas had all the b*tches back then.

They dressed clean—never bummy or shabby. Kept on the flyest shit. Suited and booted at every function, especially the clubs. The functions were poppin' back then, too—the Mr. Brickhouse and Mrs. Brickhouse contests, the Holiday Inn Holi-Dome.

Mr. Dee's had closed and changed ownership. It was now called Brown's Paradise Lounge on Stockton Boulevard. Oak Park would always had multiple nightspots and underground after-hour joints.

The nightlife was vibrant and lively. And I was trying to emulate these niggas—their moves, their ways, their words, and their actions.

CHAPTER EIGHT

"The willingness to change strategy is a fundamental requirement of an intelligent community engaged in a protracted struggle against an enemy".

\- Manu Ampim

As I was maturing mentally, I not only began rejecting the legitimacy of America's social, economic, and political institutions—I started embracing everything America rejected. At that time in my life, I didn't fully understand why I identified as a nigga or as a gangsta, why I was such a myrmidon of what amounted to ignorance.

It was only later in life—after sincere introspection, cathartic transformation, and systematic erudition—that I realized I had developed a pathological rejection of authority figures and society as a whole.

Politically speaking, as a young blood representing myself as a nigga and embracing what I didn't fully comprehend, I was unknowingly assuming a political disposition—rejecting an institution of policies and politics that my experience had already convinced me had rejected me and my kind.

You see, no matter how ignominious the attitude of a nigga may seem, it is the embodiment of a political stance—largely due to existential anxiety toward systematic class and racial oppression at the hands of our former slave masters. This is evidenced, in part, by the way, the word nigga evolved into a so-called term of endearment, expressed among a large percentage of the impoverished underclass—and even other ethnic groups beyond ours.

And yet, despite that, Black people remain on the lowest rung of the social ladder when it comes to racist subjugation—a subject I will get into later in this narrative.

But as I was saying before, I was coming up, and the hood was crackin'. I was running with real niggas—niggas who were bound to become factors in this game that never loves you back. Brothers who would leave their mark as street legends—on the track, on the field, in the arena where this game is played. These were the cats who put sharp corners on the square.

Masterminds like my close friend Anthony Cannon—one of the richest, if not the richest nigga to ever come up out of Oak Park. And trust me, there have been plenty. But none of 'em did it like him—none did it as big or as smooth.

A.C. was the first of my generation to drag a million-plus dollars up out the game. And he did it with style and finesse—like a real P. nigga should.

Legends like Terril Robinson—one of my best friends and my child's mother's relative. Or my brother from another mother, Shawn Collins, and his brother—my brother too—Big Insane, aka Nigel Collins. Shawn was one of my mentors—a good brother, loyal to those loyal to him.

Levall Murphy, Carl Royce Murphy, Leon Murphy, Greg Murphy, Eric Murphy, Big Walter (Woo) Golston, Charlie Bonton, Big Virgil, Pimpin' Bob, and Jr., his bro. All these brothers are and were my niggas—solid dudes, real niggas. My brother from another mother, Talton Robinson, was also one of my road dogs and partners in crime at this time. A lifelong friend.

I went to Peter Lassen Jr. High School—this was before California changed its schooling policies to middle schools. Back then, P.L., as we called it, was 7th, 8th, and 9th grade. This was a live-ass school—big as hell. Easily over 4,000 students.

I went to school with a gang of fast-ass b*tches. Tina Hunter, Lanna Rule Gaitol, Zoritha May, Susan Cane, Cecelia Smith, and her sisters—just to name a few. I had turned out that year, '79, running with Frankie Robinson, Leon Jordan, Athan Phillips, and Stephen Miles—who went to Kit Carson, not too far away.

We were smoking big weed in the hallways and in the bathrooms. And those bathrooms? They were crackin'.

Niggas were in there shooting dice, shaking suckas' pockets when they came in to use the bathroom, while us hoodlums were lurking, looking for a victim.

I used to carry a big-ass knife to school inside my leather three-quarter-length coat. My sister Sharon had brought it back from Hawaii as a gift, at my request—me being the devious delinquent that I was. I was a nasty lil' muthafucka too—finger-fucking lil' b*tches in the hallway between classes.

I had started chasing after Shanie Rai McFalls—a lil' fast girl, a year older than me. But I was already movin' and shakin' with the big boys. Shanie was tall and fine with that natural beauty that turned heads. She liked me on the low—definitely a PYT back then. She's the mother of my twin boys, Bryan and Brandon. You could see her shape in every pair of jeans she wore, and being young and wild, I was always on her bumper. She was seeing one of my relatives at the time, but I wasn't phased. In The P, things were just like that—folks moved how they moved. Me and my relative Carl Webb would hit licks, break bread at Shanie's house, and let her and her mother hold the food stamps.

A couple of years later, they started building the apartments on 4th Avenue. Checkmate Market was open on Broadway then—it had just moved from down on 4th Avenue a few months earlier.

I was still running with a whole community of goons—Stacy Goodson, Demetrius Jones, Steve Martinez, just to name a few. I was smoking that dookie stick—aka Sherm, aka PCP—with my relative Hot (Zilla), Big Q, Duncan Hawkins, Darren Duncan, and Conrad Usher.

And I was squabbin' a lot. Being a ghetto child, running wild. I had no real restrictions—so long as I checked in with Mom, tapped in, and let her know I was with one of my folks, it was good.

My relative Hot had just turned out. He was 17 and already pimping the blood out of Janice Felix (Nasty). She had chose up and was stomping down for him. He had knocked her from Houston—though, a few years later, Big Walt put tips on him for not respecting the rules of the game. Hot felt some type of way about it.

I was trying to get mine, too—trying to fuck Lanna's fast, tall ass. I was getting taller myself, hanging with Stephanie Miles, Scooby, Kevin Stringfellow, and Chris Hardway—a.k.a. Hardrock. I was messing around with this girl, Julie—light-skinned, young, and wild. She was feeling me heavy, and I was feeling myself—young, reckless, thinking I was grown. Sneaking in her window, making it happen.

Stephen Miles had put me up on game regarding her loose moral character. She was letting Scooby hit, too.

Scooby and Stephen went to Kit Carson with a gang of other homies—Leroy Woods and Kevin Stringfellow, just to name a few.

My homie Herman Thomas was living off 10th Avenue by Stockton Boulevard. His two sisters, Missy and Candy, were whoopin' niggas' asses. They would beat up on niggas for real up at P.L.—before, during, and after school. But they were always cool with me. We're still cool to this day. I thought they were cute too.

Around this time, I was running with Hardrock and Talton Robinson. I was one of the first in my peer group to own a firearm. I had a cut-down 12-gauge.

I was about 12 years old, already 6'1" or 6'2". It didn't matter—I looked 18. We were out doing robberies. I'd carry hella shells in my 501 jeans, the handle wrapped in black electrical tape.

Hot used to be part of one of the hardest pop-locking groups in Sacramento and the Bay Area—Precise Device. Them niggas would hit on a dime. Then you had Mechanical Wizards, The Derby Dancers, and The Prime Ministers. But none of them could fuck with the homies.

Hot, Big Q, Tony Flaff, Benji, and a few others would dance at the California State Fair. They turned that thang out. A group from West Oakland, Derek, and Company, would battle the homies at the newly built convention center downtown.

Oak Park also had a raw-ass female dance troupe called SSL—Soul Sisters Incorporated. They did their thang, too. Then there were The Discoletes, a drill team known for their bold routines—shaking it heavy, all in sync. This was Patty Parker's group, with D.D. Taylor and a few other solid females. Patty was legendary in the hood—she had a figure that turned heads from every block, thick and built like no other.

When they did that Freeze-Do-It routine? Those hips were shaking left to right. Ha! Ha! A gang of ass was shaking back then.

Not long after this, my brother Jerome got released from **CYA (California Youth Authority)**. He had been down about a year or so. I was excited—anxious to kick it with him.

Lil' James had just shot back to Denver, Colorado, so Jerome coming home meant we could run it up. We kicked it hard blew some weed. Nigga punched on me a few times, told me I was getting big—which I was. Asked me if I had a female on my line. All that big brother shit.

But he ended up heading to Denver to stay out the way. It was slower up there at the time.

Meanwhile, I had to make the gun fat enough to hold when I fired it. It was short and had a big kick. I had 00-aught caliber shells. I'd shoot trash cans in the Big Park at night or let off rounds in Scooby's backyard on 40th, off of 11th Avenue.

Took that thang over to Fat Kev's joint on 33rd Street. We were just kids, man. Babies in the woods, but man-children. This was Oak Park.

Twelve was seventeen or sixteen—depending on the household you were raised in. One thing was certain—nobody was slow. Violence was normalized because we knew nothing else.

I was on 4th Avenue daily back then, before they built the apartments that stand there now. Before the apartments, it was just a field, a merry-go-round, dirt, and broken glass. The Paradons stayed across the street on San Jose Way. The homie Dog Charlie was fucking with their mother. Dog Charlie was one of the biggest pimps of that era. Shit was live too.

I used to kick it with Deaf Donald Paradon—he was my big bro Jerome's road dog back then. We kicked it at the park, drinking Old English, blowing that gold weed, and drinking Thunderbird too. Then, everything changed.

Jerome was accidentally killed by a gunshot to the chest. I was devastated. I found out while I was at my Aunt Beulah's joint on 2nd Avenue. We went to Denver to lay him to rest.

Me and Hot got into it after the funeral. We blew some coke before the homegoing service—down in the basement of Aunt Payne's joint in the Five Points community in Denver. Hot was fucking with me. And me being a lil' manish nigga, I was buckin' the system.

We had also checked some suckas at McDonald's earlier that day. They were playing with the game but didn't want no problems. By this time, I was getting tall as hell—growing up fast. I knew how to hold my composure, wasn't running around grinning and shit.

My family? They were always lacing my boots—making me tougher, stronger, smarter, sharper. My street education was every day. Because I was born in it. I wasn't looking at the game from the outside. I was ten toes deep in it. Every cat I ran with was older than me.

When I returned to Sac, my relative Detchie had caught a case in L.A. It was off a lick they had hit—fucking around on the track. But they got jacked by the rollers.

My big relly Darrel Smith was getting hoe money too at this time. He was twenty toes down. Had a Lac. A '69 Impala. Sending hoes out to get his trap right.

CHAPTER NINE

The hood was live! Clubs were jumpin' all up and down Stockton Blvd. Mr. Dee's had closed down, and the homie Dante Drayton was stabbed to death up there by the other homie Darren Paradon, who was just a juvenile at the time—only 14 or 15 years old—but already knee-deep in the game. In fact, the whole Paradon family was about that life.

It was hoin' going on! And a lot of pimping and pandering. You could smell the PCP at P. Funk's joint on 33rd and 10th Ave. He had a duplex across 33rd, right before you got to 12th Ave. Had the whole street smelling like Sherm! That "Butt Naked"—so-called because fools would come up out their clothes on that shit. They would run down the street naked. That Angel Dust was crackin', too. Dust was poppin' before Sherm hit, though.

Any drug you could think of was in Oak Park. Hop (heroin), and coke were being pumped into balloons up at the Big Park—$10 sacks of both for the speedballers, $20 too. You could have your way as long as you had the cash to partake—right there in the park, in broad daylight, seven days a week. My whole hood was crackin'.

We have always been on some get-money shit. For as long as I've been alive—and even before that—Oak Park was about getting paper. Period.

Rainbow Bakery, at this time, was facing 33rd St.—this was before it got rebuilt in the late '70s and early '80s and before McGeorge School of Law started buying up all the property along 33rd St. to extend their school and add parking structures. Back when the Oak Park Library— right there on 5th Ave. and 33rd St.—was our community library. Dave's Soul Center was still on 33rd back then, too, before you hit Broadway.

So, back then, the old bakery was still open. It was just an old building, 50 to 60 years old at the time, sitting right across the street from the Big Park. In the summertime, after we were done swimming at the park when the pool had closed down, we used to go over to the bakery—hella deep. Walter Anderson, Donnie Pitts, Leander Cook, and many more—just to name a few.

We'd just kick open the door to the bakery and take all that shit. We were up in that thang. You could smell the bread being baked—then, just like you can now.

They had an old-school burglar alarm—a red box high up on the outside wall of the bakery. That shit would ring, but the police didn't come. There were no McGeorge School of Law patrols back then.

That fresh-baked bread, cupcakes, and shit? It was like a magnet to all of us ghetto kids.

We were famished from swimming all day in that 100-degree Sacramento heat—the kind of heat that's typical of all Sacramento summers.

There would be as many as 30 or 40 kids running up in that old bakery, snatching cupcakes and all kinds of sweets. Most of us had the munchies. And we didn't respect the establishment because they didn't do shit for the community. They just took our money and never gave anything back. That old bakery never stood a chance.

Understand—this was right after the civil rights movement of the 1960s. Sacramento was still extremely racist in its policies and directives when it came to communities of color. Shit, they still are.

We looked at everything as us against them. And them? They were the white racist establishment. Them crackers in Sac spent millions of taxpayer dollars patrolling, harassing, and locking up people of color—mainly from Del Paso Heights and Oak Park. For decades, they did this.

Even the RT city buses would stop running down 5th Ave. and 33rd St. at 6:00 P.M.—because of the neighborhood. RT (Regional Transit) is the city bus company. No buses ran down those streets after dark. But they still rolled down Broadway—it was bright enough for the drivers to feel safe.

If I had to take an educated guess, it's because no trees obscured the view on Broadway. Oak Park was a dangerous place at night. And you know the freaks come out at night. The streets were black as pitch back then—super dark because of the abundance of oak trees in this part of the city.

The Mid City District—which Oak Park is a part of—was Sacramento's first suburb. The city planners planted oak trees everywhere to help keep this part of the city cool in the hot summers.

Every avenue and street in Oak Park has a bunch of shade trees lining both sides. Some of these trees are over 100 years old, maybe even older. They shade the streets and keep the community cooler than other parts of the city, but at night, they make the avenues pitch black. We got a lot of shade in more ways than one.

For example, the California State Fair used to be located in Oak Park—right at Stockton Blvd. and Broadway, where the DMV office is now. It was later moved to the northeast section of the city. I learned to ride my first bike in the empty lots of the old state fairgrounds.

White flight took the fair out of Oak Park.

They moved it to a more "family-friendly environment."

Our community was basically cut off from the rest of the city when they built the freeway in 1962—Highway 99. It divided the white folks from us, turning Oak Park into a self-contained unit. A Jim Crow move—right here in Cali.

At the time, County Hospital was called The Medical Center—now it's UCD Medical Center. I shot my first firearm in a field right next to the hospital, which was also part of the old fairgrounds. Later on, they built a 7-Eleven right next to UCD Medical Center.

The nightlife in Oak Park was thriving back then.

Springer's Liquor Store sat right on Broadway, where Food Source is now. There was also a gas station, a gambling shack, and behind Springer's, an area called The Log—where the winos and dope fiends hung out. Drinking, shooting dope—all manner of getting high.

Heroin was being sold back there on The Log.

Shit was grimy.

The whole area reeked of urine. Broken glass covered the ground. Used needles scattered everywhere. I used to break bottles myself back there after I finished my Old English 800 quarts of malt liquor.

I was a lil' ghetto boy.

If you weren't from Oak Park, you did not want to get caught behind Springer's. Monsters lurked there.

As a young blood, me and my lil' gang of toughs ran up in Springer's, taking so much merchandise. Myself, Talton Orson, Shy, Bobo, Conrad— just to name a few. We were young hoodlums, snatching up beer, wine, and anything else we could get our hands on.

We hit them so many times that they eventually put chicken wire all over the store's entrance—right by the doorway.

The inside of the store ended up looking like a baby prison. You couldn't just walk in and grab what you wanted. You had to step up to the counter and ask Old Man Will to grab what you needed.

There was a whole section inside the store that was blocked off. You had to point at what you wanted, and Will would retrieve it and bring it to the counter. We were some bad lil' muthafuckas. Terrible actors— inside and outside of our native community.

Across the street from Springer's was the Joy Riders Car Club. The Body Language Nightclub was poppin' back then, too. Anderson's Liquor Store was on the corner of 8th Ave. and Stockton Blvd.

Years later, I would be involved in a major gun battle—right in front of Springer's. Broad daylight. Some hood shit. As usual, no police cared. No police came. This was the hood. The police never came. But I'm getting ahead of the narrative—bear with me.

At this time, Oak Park had a day face and a night face. Both were equally menacing. The streets were alive—all day, all night. Especially if you knew where to look. There were plenty of nooks and crannies up in that place to be. Niggas were getting money. Paper was flowing.

At the time, I was still living on 36th St., off 12th Ave., around the corner from Mrs. Harris, Fat Gregory, Jamal, and Leslie Taylor. My homie Jeff (Baily) lived across the street in the duplexes with his two sisters, Kimmie and Rina. Sissy lived on the corner of 10th Ave. We would eventually buy that house some years later. Yvonne and Lisa and their lil' bro, Austin, lived across the street from us.

The Washingtons—Chill Will, Andre, and their lil' sister Lisa— lived down the street on 10th, up the street from Mama Joyce—my folks, too. Mama Joyce was Uncle Big Floyd's sister. I had a whole lotta folks on that street, in that area. Tracy's lil' nasty ass stayed on 35th, right in the back of my street. Tow Truck Joe had a house on 35th, too. He and my Uncle Jimmy grew up together. This was all before they built Oak Park Market on 12th Ave.

At this time, we would go downtown, hella deep on Sundays, to the movies on K Street Mall—aka the Esquire Theater—and the Crest Theater before it got re-rocked into the IMAX joint it is now. We'd be almost 100 deep, or at least it felt that way. It seemed like the whole teenage population was down at the movies on Sundays.

Some of us came by bus, others got dropped off, but either way, it was all hood up in that joint. Oak Park niggas, females, and even girls from other parts of the city.

We were smoking big weed up in there—right in the theater during the shows. As soon as you walked in, the smell of marijuana would hit you right in the nose. The smoke would hit you in the face.

Back then, you could still smoke cigarettes in most establishments. Security at the theater wouldn't fuck with us because there were too many of us. Plus, we were spending hella money on food at the snack bar. That theater was raggedy—in various states of disrepair—but they were making tons of money off us ghetto kids. We'd converge, congregate, and partake in all kinds of illegal activities.

I remember one time, someone threw an empty Hennessy bottle and hit one of the ushers—or maybe a security guard. They ran up in there on us. Walter Anderson told them straight up to mind their muthafuckin' business and leave us the fuck alone. They left us alone. There were way too many of us for them to be fucking with.

We'd be up in that thang fitted, too—Stacy Adams shoes, leather coats, golf hats with the pins we got from Joe's Style Shop downtown. Burner gloves, derby hats, stingy brims. Hot used to rock this black and white beaver hat—he copped it in Oakland at Eastmont Mall. All black, with the white trim. This was the end of the '70s.

I saw all the Blaxploitation flicks—The Mack, Superfly—at the Esquire. Some I saw at the Colonial Theater in Oak Park too. But these films didn't teach me anything. I knew real macks and real superflies—in living color, right in my hood. I saw these cats daily, handling their business—foxin', gettin' it with the crooks. We also watched hella kung fu flicks at The Star Theater. They made big money off us kids.

I saw Seven Deadly Venoms there, along with a gang of Bruce Lee flicks. At the time, we were all into martial arts. It was kung fu instead of hip-hop. That underdog, rise-up mentality in kung fu flicks resonated with most of us in the New Afrikan community.

The soundtrack of our lives at this time? Parliament, Funkadelic, Bootsy Collins, Brides of Funkenstein, Bernie Worrell, James Brown, Brass Construction, B.T. Express, The Whispers, Brothers Johnson,

Ohio Players, The O'Jays, Earth, Wind & Fire, Brick, Slave, Lakeside, Rick James.

All things funk. All things funky. Hip-hop had yet to take root on the West Coast. It would later become the soundtrack for Generation X— but at that time, we were Gen X, and in my case, Generation Malcolm X. That music? It was the expression rising from the ashes of The Black Souls. A street would emerge and wreak havoc.

Its base of operations? Wall Street—7th Ave. and 37th Street— extending to 12th Ave. and 37th Street—the Mad Pad. At this time, Oak Park Market had yet to be built on 12th Ave. Same with the KFC on Broadway and Alhambra Blvd.—that spot was just being built. We robbed that KFC so much they ended up installing bulletproof glass all along the front counter.

They built it so secure that you had to put your money into a bulletproof glass box that swiveled—no contact with the cashier. You got your order the same way—through that swivel box. The owners of that KFC saw it as "selling chicken to Black folks." It would always be a profit-making franchise.

Cold thang. These crackers were selling slow death—strokes, heart disease—to our people. The same way they do now. Meanwhile, the police acted like a military occupying force in our community. The same way they still do in New Afrikan communities nationwide. We had a hostile relationship with law enforcement—if any relationship at all.

At night? The police would not come to Oak Park. They wouldn't send one patrol car, one officer. They'd drive down 8th Ave. or 7th Ave. at night, see all the Afrikans on the streets, and just turn around—or drive through at high speed, right past the crowd. They ignored all the illegal shit going on. They paid it no mind.

CHAPTER TEN

At this juncture in Oak Park history, the most dominant street tribe was the Funk Lords. The YG's were the Touch Hogs—these boys were vicious knockout artists. Fools were getting knocked out at every function or venue they showed up at. They showed up and showed out. This was the "must bust" era—a time just before the crack era.

Then came the O.P.B.C.—the Oak Park Busta Crabber era. The Wall Street Bust era. Even the Wall Street Bust, a two-step dance, was created in the hood, by the hood.

Every house party we went to in South Sacramento back then, we rolled in caravans—20, 30 cars deep. Sometimes, even 60 or 70 of us would crash the same party. And before the night was over, somebody was getting knocked out and stomped out. 99.9% of the time, it was somebody not from the community.

It was inevitable. Somebody would yell "BUST!"—and right then and there, it was on and crackin'. We'd turn out the party and move on to the next one. And at the next function? Somebody was getting busted on in succession.

We had knockout artists. One-punch niggas like Kenny Lee, Darrel Williams, Donnie Pitts, Duncan Hawkins, Leevall Murphy. I personally witnessed Leevall knock out so many muthafuckas. It was ridiculous. And he wasn't even a big dude—just really athletic. He would beat fools mercilessly—knocking them out so hard, they'd be pissing themselves.

A true knockout artist.

Niggas like Toney Bean, Gerald Bean, Ronnie Robinson, James Usher, Frank Davis, Big K.P., Clemmie Fields, Tony Smith—way too many to list. I could write a whole book about the niggas from the hood at this time who were sleeping fools all over the city.

That era is long gone. Ain't no more fighting. That shit went the way of the dinosaurs. This was Oak Park's golden age. We will never see those times again. But I hope we rebuild that hood love again—we need it now more than ever. That self-love, instead of self-serving hate.

When the mini-series Roots came out—based on the book by Alex Haley—we were going up to Hughes Stadium for football games at night and knocking out white boys on general principle.

Just because we were finally being subjected to the truth about the devil and his crimes against us, against humanity. If you got caught slippin' up at Hughes Stadium during a Sac High football game and you were a cracker, you were tipped. Period.

No questions asked. Just knocked out. This was Oak Park. And we were accustomed to being mistreated by the powers that be in our city. We were equal opportunity when it came to whooping ass—anybody not from our community was fair game. We would be so deep walking back from Hughes Stadium—multiple groups of 40, 50, 20 people or more. An intimidating sight.

If you were white, you did not want to be caught in the park after dark or anywhere near Oak Park after dark. This was the legacy of the 1940s, 1950s, and the turbulent 1960s—years of racist policies and practices by the ones who wielded all the power to enact and enforce unjust laws in Sacramento.

If caught over that dividing line, you were whooped and robbed. Back then, Rio Linda, a white community in North Sac, had the KKK and would do marches and spew racist shit in the media. I, as always, would be the youngest eyes observing the goings on with my brothers and older relatives, seeing this shit first hand. We would have huge gatherings back then in William Land park on Sundays. There would be literally hundreds of people, sometimes thousands, depending on the vibe and what was going on at the time. All the bad b*tches would be up there, ass on display, hips, lips, and fingertips on hit. Sometimes, we would go right to the park after the movies. In the spring and summer months, this was the place to be and be seen especially every Easter Sunday. This was when all the park stalls were available and you could park in the back of Fairy Tale Town.

All the parking stalls would be filled with vehicles, music bumping, barbecuing, dice games, the whole nine yards. And without fail, somebody was getting knocked out or hit with a bumper jack, oftentimes before the event was over. It was usually Oak Park making that noise and talking that fuss to them fuck boys and suckas. As it would happen, the Funk Lords and Touch Hogs would be a big part of Oak Park's street organization history.

We used to wear blue and black flags back in the day and had always referred to each other as blood. We wore kung fu gi's and would go to every function hella deep and serve anybody who didn't like that we were up in the spot letting our nuts drag the ground.

Wall Street and Mad Pad were headquarters.

Taco Rico was cracking—bomb-ass Mexican food. Ray and Juanita owned Taco Rico, right there on MLK (Sacramento Blvd.) and Broadway. We all grew up eating Taco Rico.

Checkmate Market? It was burned down for the insurance money at its second location on Broadway, behind the apartments on 4th Ave... The owners later rebuilt it right at the corner of 38th and Broadway— where the Record Tree Music Store used to be. Record Tree was the spot back in the '70s.

The owners of Checkmate Market got rich off Wall Street. The store was right on the corner of a dope track—they made money selling malt liquor, Newport, Camel non-filters, rolling papers, Players Magazines, and everything else the hood needed.

I used to be knocked out on the floor in Randy Moses's spot, top of Wall Street, high as a giraffe's pussy, sleeping off my Old E and weed high. I was fucking with Wayne Moses. Back then, I was busting down pounds of weed over at Reggie Prince's joint with my big homie Willie Archie—a stomp-down gangsta.

As a young blood, I was running the streets with Chilly Will (Willard Cochran). His sister, Tanya Jackson, was my sister's best friend back then. She had a lot of friends—cute girls, popular girls. Mia Mitchell, Lee Lee Bennet, Christine Berry, Dee Dee Taylor, Leslie Taylor—too many to list. I could write a small novel just about all the females who used to spend the night at our house back then.

I was in the streets with Chill, Clemmie Fields, Ronnie Fields (Peg Leg), Hard Rock, my relly Carl Webb, S.D. The hood was live. If you were a sucka or a punk, you couldn't have shit. Like in any inner-city situation or any ghetto in Amerikkka, if you were soft, your shit got taken. Period.

Bikes, clothes, shoes—whatever. Especially money. By this time, I was coming into my own. My relly Detchie and Darrel had a spot on 3rd Ave.—a bachelor pad, if you will. Troy Allen—not New Boy (the original Troy Allen), but the Troy Allen from the Bay Area—was there, too. They would all be over there on 3rd Ave., kickin' it.

Meanwhile, New Boy was running with my relly Hot. They had just been caught up in a riot at Hughes Stadium during a track meet. Shit got heated, and they put hands and feet on some white folks. It was all over the news. It even made the Sacramento Bee and the Sacramento Union. Big news in the town.

Now, Sacramento only has one newspaper. But back then, one of the oldest Black newspapers—The Sacramento Observer—was still around.

They might have reported on the incident, too, since The Observer was located in Oak Park, right off 35th St. and 6th Ave.

At the time, Duncan Hawkins, Big Q, Hot, Walter Anderson, and New Boy were moving reckless. New Boy—the youngest in the cadre—was about to turn 18. Niggas were out here doing dumb shit. But I looked up to these cats. They were my extended family. And I was about to make my name in the underworld soon enough…

At this juncture in my Quran (history), I was just doing the knowledge. Looking, learning, observing, respecting the game. We were about to bring 4th Avenue to life. Soon, there was a lil' weed spot pumping dime bags only. This was Cripple Rob's spot—in the newly constructed apartments on 4th Ave. Rob was in a wheelchair. Hippy, Grover, and O.G. Reggie had this spot on the Ave. first. This was the first money-making machine on 4th Avenue—the second apartment from the back. And this was bomb weed. Fire. No dirt. Just Kush.

Meanwhile, The Barrons had that water (PCP) on 3rd Ave.—Jackie, Freddie, and lil' bro Randy Barron. You could smell that wet as soon as you turned off San Jose Way and hooked that left on 3rd. Shit was LOUD back then, too. Real water. Not that watered-down shit we got now. This was Gorilla Piss. One-hitter-quitter.

My Auntie's house was on The Deuce (2nd Ave.). That was the location of the infamous Honeycomb Hideout—the basement of her house. The Big Park was still an epicenter of activity. We had The Urban League—a sponsored school next to the Big Park called Inner City. Eventually, they would put the Police Athletic League (PAL) boxing gym there. Inner City served free lunch all summer long. That was needed—because most of the kids lived below the poverty line.

This was the legacy of the Black Panther Party's Free Breakfast Programs. Baseball was booming up at The Big Park, too—part of the fabric of our community. Coaches like Mr. Crump, Mr. Blackwell, Mr. Bullard, and O.G. Howard were out there every year—from T-Ball to Seniors.

My big homie, Junie Darden, was my first baseball coach. Shit was live. Food cookin', music bumpin'—shit smellin' good. Fools hustlin', money movin'—a hustlin' and bustlin' environment every weekend, all spring and summer long. We were family. But shit was about to change. A menace was coming to every ghetto in Amerikkka. It would affect us all. And it still is…

CHAPTER ELEVEN

O.P.G

———⟳———

So, there were real live hitters in the hood at this time, just like there are now. Back then, you had real G's like Blue Felix, Freddie Washington, Raymond Washington, Leon Murphy, Leevall Murphy, Carl Murphy, Eric Murphy, Doug Wayne, Tony Ellis, Base Pipe Mike, Pete Brown, JoJo Waters, Dennis Miller, Tony Allen, Shawn Collins, and Leander Cook. Most of the latter, along with many of the above, were mentors of mine. Then you had Charlie Bonton, Ronnie Robinson, Ice Water, Big Blake, Dirty Eran, also known as Earnest Johnson, Big Tree Top, Ray Dick, Duncan Hawkins, Junk Yard, John Earl, and Big David Towner—just to name a few.

Around this time, one of my older homies went down south to LA County—Pomona, California. The San Gabriel Valley was a bit slow and out of the way at the time, but he was bank robbing down there. A lot of my folks from Oak Park migrated to Pomona as well, and they took our game with them. It was from this migration that PCP, the Water, was introduced to Sacramento around 1975 or 1976. One of my brothers from another mother brought this game back to Sac. My folks also

47

caught a case out in Pomona—some hot shit in '76—and came back home a couple of years later.

That same year, my homie Tony Allen caught a double homicide in Compton. A Crip boy was out there shouting his hood, busting his gun—something we did not do in the P. So, in effect, he was identifying himself. The homie was told where to find him, and when he got the drop, he busted his shit for playing. Our wet work was usually done without the fanfare.

After these two cats came home from CYA for these homicides, they returned to Sacramento. My brothers from another mother, Shawn and Nigel Collins, were back in town. Their mother, Merlene, was living in the south area on Newport. Shawn had just flipped a Lincoln Town Car, clean as fuck. Some bustas cocktailed it in front of Merlene's spot on Newport. We used to fight with them cats out south, and after we got on some fools out there, that was their way of getting back.

I was getting a raw double dose of game from all of my older homies—Shawn and Big Tone. I was running hard with my Ace, Talton Robinson. We had just had one of our folks get shot at Springer's Liquor Store—some in-hood shit. Watching it all unfold in slow motion, just like a movie, drinking a Squirt soda water.

By this time, I was used to gun violence. It was commonplace in my community, like the Wild West. I also remember one of the homies being stabbed to death as soon as he entered Vacaville State Prison—over some bullshit. Over a b*tch. Over some pussy that wasn't even his.

He had been jumping on this female, breaking her for her paper on some gorilla shit. And as soon as he hit Vacaville, them goons were waiting on that ass. Two P. niggas—killers in their own right—brutally took him out as he was coming out of the church house. They got away smooth. This was his first day of movement in the joint.

This wouldn't be the first time, nor the last, that I would see or hear about a fool getting his birthdate taken over some pussy that wasn't his.

Over some dumb shit. Pussy or disrespect could send you home in a box. The game was like that—it did not suffer fools.

Justice is a penalty or a reward for one's actions. I was told that in my wonder years, and would eventually serve a lot of justice myself.

This was the game in its purest form at that time. This was when maxi coats had just gone out of fashion—that era was over. All things change.

Mr. Dee's had closed and was reopened by another cat named Mr. Brown. He renamed the club Brown's Paradise Lounge. Mr. Brown had been a cook at Old Folsom Prison—a prison I used to visit as a child and preteen in the early '70s to see my relatives. That same prison would one day play a big part in my education.

Brown's Paradise Lounge was now the spot on Stockton Blvd. They threw big player shit up there—pimps and their hoes would show off, the nightlife was all the way live, and money was everywhere. Boosting, gambling—anything and everything was being bought and sold in Oak Park. You name it, we had it—or we could get it. Period.

The big homies had a flock of go-getting b*tches sockin' it to their pockets. They had thievin' ass hoes, too. These cats were living the sporting life—major players like David Towner, D.W., Donnie Pitts, Tree Top, and Big Rudy Henderson. These brothers were cross-country pimps and major macks—and pimping and macking is exactly what they did. They took this game from The Big Apple to The Pineapple. Man, these niggas was having paper.

I was soakin' up game on every dope spot, every corner, every gamblin' spot, and every after-hours joint I could get into. You name it, I was there if there was game being disseminated. I was on the "Hoe" corner on 9th Ave and 33rd St. It would be at least 60 or 70 of us on that corner back in the day or around that corner. 33rd St is a major thoroughfare running the heart of Oak Park. A two-way street going north and south, this street would birth a major team of money-getters. Thorough players, thorough b*tches, and hittas, all of them growing up on that street or off

49

that street. Roland Hawkins from the Mad Pad still had spot rolling on 33rd. Roland had just copped his 'Lac a Sedan De'Ville light gold it was clean. I used to sit in Donnie Pitt's town car on the hoe corner, chopping game and getting laced. He would give me the ins and outs of this game, all facets of it.

Smoking that gold weed and drinking beer we got from Tom's Market right there on 33rd.and 9th. I remember when Donnie copped that town car, it was gun-metal gray. It was the latest model he bought in the year it came out. He got it out a hoe's ass, hoe money. Donnie stayed in L.A., getting his traps right at this time. He kept 30 to 40 toes down at all times. Stompin' down that is on that track nigga was official. Being an Oak Park nigga his game was executed at a high-performance level. The cat was official on any mutha fuckin' Martin Luther King. This was before they had MLK's in every ghetto USA. Sacramento Blvd was still just that.

This was the environment that shaped my mind and developed my perspective. These streets had a profound effect on my psyche. They were harsh conditions, unforgiving, much like life itself. I would learn from these streets that men of prey should only compete with themselves. I would become a product of my environment, and in due time, like fruit that grows in its season, my environment would become a product of me. Myself and those of my generation would change these streets and define them for generations to come—after this first X generation.

My peers would change these streets for good in the next decade. For now, though, I was doing dumb shit—learning, growing, changing, getting this game raw, right, and exact. I was born in it, as opposed to those who are late bloomers. I took to it like a duck takes to water. The air was alive with kinetic energy, and I was all in it. An outsider would get ate up in my hood at this time. There was no crack, no rap, but there was sex, money, and murder. Powder coke, heroin, PCP, speed, weed, pills—the whole alphabet soup of drugs from A to Z.

Me and my niggas ran these streets from sunup to sunup again, from can't see to can't see again. I was knee-deep in it at this moment in time with my dog Conrad Usher, my big homie John Usher's son, who had just moved back from St. Louis. His brother G.P. would become a lifelong friend of mine. Conrad was living on 4th Ave with his grandmother, Ms. Usher, who was like a mother to me, too.

Genaro Patterson would become a true brother from another mother. That is his honorable name, but we've called him G.P. since we were kids on the block—Four Black, or Foe Block, as we affectionately called headquarters. G.P. is Tiny Tim's brother, and they also had another brother named Bunkin, also known as Charles Patterson. Bunkin used to run with my big bro James back in the day.

Me, G.P., and Conrad would blow big weed, listen to Blow Fly, and chase money and fast-ass b*tches who were out of pocket in the hood. All that good young adolescent shit we all do coming of age. Having hella fun riding G.P.'s moped—he had just got that thang, money green. He would ride it from the Heights to the P, and that would inspire me and my relly Carl Webb to go snatch one of our own up at Florin Mall. We had to liberate that thang from some sucka who was less deserving of it at the time.

The game was live and good. My bro "lil James" taught me how to use a knife in a fight back then, which would actually come in handy a few times in my life. I don't think my brothers and relatives—Darrel, Detchie, Hot, John Earl—knew they were creating a super predator by lacing my boots and tying my laces the way they did.

CHAPTER TWELVE

—◦—

I would learn all the skills needed to survive in my concrete jungle from my big homies and extended family. At this point, we were all family up in that Oak Park village.

I went to California Middle School after it was changed from a junior high in 1979. I had gotten kicked out of Peter Lassen Jr. High for whoopin' on this white b*tch—the teacher's aide in my gym class. I went to California Middle School after it was changed from a junior high in 1979. I had gotten kicked out of Peter Lassen Jr. High for whoopin' on this white girl—the teacher's aide in my gym class. My older homie, Dino Johnson, had grabbed her backside—she was a ninth grader had some curves on her, nothing major. He did that bold move right in front of me, and she turned around and swung on me like I did it.

I ducked it and slapped the fire out of her. Clipboard went flying. That was it for me—got kicked out for that incident. It was the final straw in a long list of me putting hands on folks at that school. Typical ghetto child shit. I went to Cal—as it was called—with my good friends Kevin Hooks, Kirk Crump, Shawn Powells, Chris Hobson, Stephen Gray, Anthony Cannon, Fat Bobo, Walton, and his sister Toni. My sister Felicia, my relative Kevin "Flashlight" Chaney, Mia Mitchell, Christine

Berry, Kenny Graham, Brook Pitts, Kenny Pitts—shit, it was a gang of us.

We were all bussed to Cal because our junior high had burned down in the late '60s, and the crackers didn't want to rebuild it. They didn't want to spend money in our community.

We caught the school bus on 18th Ave., behind Oak Park Market. A bunch of us would take beer out of the trucks parked at the market while they were restocking in the morning—around 6:30 or 7:00 AM.

They had just built the store, and I guess they didn't know that you couldn't just leave the side of the truck open while you wheeled cases of beer inside. This was The P. We were opportunists. And that opportunity was exploited constantly—until they wised up and started locking that thang up early in the morning, knowing the natives were on their way to school.

We would drink the beer before getting on the bus—downing cans smoking weed—all at 12 and 13 years old. Oak Park Market was built on a vacant lot that once housed a long-defunct gas station—abandoned due to white flight in the early '60s or earlier. Me and, Fat Kev would be snorting powder coke on the back of the bus before school. It was just us back there. No dorks allowed. I already had a hammer on me. We wore Stacy Adams, baggies, leather coats, and golf hats from Joe's Style Shop. The pants were tweed, with pleats in the front.

A lot of our gear came from Joe's Style Shop downtown. Joe's used to have his shop in the hood, on 35th St., in the '50s and '60s, but after all the police murders, he moved to the J Street location. A lot of pimps and macks got their clothes from Joe's Style Shop—he even had a photo collage of all the prostitutes who frequented his place of business.

This was the same year Michael Jackson dropped Off the Wall— his best work, in my opinion. The same year, Rapper's Delight came out. There was a lot of good music in rotation—Cameo, The Brothers Johnson, Con Funk Shun, Sun, Slave, Parliament. A bunch of fire was out, and we were all going to Florin Skate—the skating rink in South Sac, in the back of Florin Mall.

The rink was crackin' all night long—from 7 PM to 7 AM—serving as a de facto babysitter for parents who were a little more lenient with their kids. '79 had a lot going on. Those all-night skate parties carried on into '80, but things were about to change.

Back then, fools in South Sac were considered square bears compared to us. That shit was nice out there—the houses, the streets. No alleys, no dope spots, no dope fiends scratching their arms asking for money. No used needles in the park where kids played. That shit was pristine compared to Del Paso Heights and Oak Park. The latter were true ghettos.

I had taken to smoking a lot of PCP—Sherm—back then. With my relatives, Hot, I could always handle smoking an incredible amount of PCP. It was not a problem for my mental—I acted the same and held my composure. I would blow whole sticks of Sherm at The Mad Pad on 37th, just around the corner from my house, with the Funk Lords, New Boy, Hot, Big Q, Duncan (Woodrow) Hawkins, and Mable Stringfellow— Duncan's baby mother, Marcus's mother. I remember when she had Marcus. Big Q was fucking with Gooba (Helen) Hawkins. I was messing around with Angie back then—she was a lil' fast one, thick and young. I was smashing her every night over there, caught up in that wild energy we both had at the time.

At the time, I was running with Jug Head (John Cooks), Kevin Stringfellow, Stephen Miles, Scooby, and Kenneth, who stayed on 40th off 11th Ave., across the street from Scooby. We were fucking with the skating rink, tough. I was always fighting up there, checking niggas' pockets in the bathroom when they came in playing. We were lurking up in that thang.

My relative Detchie and big homie Walter Anderson used to be outside in the parking lot. Tony Patterson used to be with them, too.

We would be deep outside and inside the rink. The parking lot would be full of cars and people. And Oak Park? We were knocking out somebody, whether it was inside or outside—but it was bound to happen. It's what we did and how we moved.

The function would get turned out. Somebody would be victimized, and their shit would get taken. All the hoodlum and hood shit. The homies were up there deeper than Atlantis—burner gloves on, hammered up in the parking lot, dressed to impress. And we were always showing up and showing out. There were no Crip street tribes at this time in Sacramento.

The South Sacramento area was known as Cabrillo Gardens, or just The Gardens. Later, it would be called Gorilla Gardens. It was originally built as Cabrillo Gardens in the early '70s, and most of the families that moved there were from Oak Park. They were first-time homebuyers looking to escape the poverty and crime of Oak Park or Del Paso Heights.

But Oak Park and Del Paso Heights never really got along with this area of the city in later years. My homie Slate Rock's family moved from Oak Park to Cabrillo Gardens in the early '70s. He would terrorize that area. Making big noise—doing home invasions on white folks who got caught slipping. Shit got so bad out there they would put the schools on lockdown if they thought Slate Rock was loose in the community. He was considered armed and dangerous. Rollers were after him for a myriad of crimes.

Meanwhile, back in the slums, the whole hood was on some get-money shit. There were bank robbery teams—Terry Washington, Steve (Stevo) Martinez, Bobo (Noel)—hitting licks left and right. G. Brown was in the mix, too. Bobo had copped a lowrider—a '61 Impala, clean as hell. They were getting down with Gangsta Pete (Sawyer) out of Shiloh Arms.

Shiloh Arms was a group of apartments owned by Shiloh Baptist Church on 9th Ave. and 36th St.—situated in East Oak Park, right behind Oak Ridge Elementary School. I used to hang out in Shiloh Arms back then. Kicking it at Gangsta Pete's joint upstairs, blowing big weed, talking big shit.

Me, Stevo, Shy, Bobo—we all posted up. I had sold my bike to Kenny Buffer for some weed back then. Kenny had a spot in Shiloh. He had a primer gray Monte Carlo and a '69—I think it was. But I could not go home without my bike. So I went and got my relative Detchie and Walter Anderson. Walt knocked on Kenny Buffer's door and said, "You got my lil' brother's bike?"

Detchie backed the blue LTD up into the parking space and popped the trunk. Kenny said, "I bought it from him, though." That whole time he was talking, he was already bringing the bike out and putting it in the walkway.

I grabbed my shit, hit the quick release on the front wheel, dropped that thang in the trunk, jumped in the car—And we bounced up outta there.

Big Walt was on some smashing shit, and the look he gave Kenny was enough to make him produce my property. Detchie was on some smashing shit, too—he was well-known back then for shooting niggas and shooting at niggas. I was just being me, a mannish lil' nigga. A Y.G. on my way to becoming something quite frightening soon enough.

It was '80 going into '81. I was in my era—the '80s. I was in love with guns and the game. What a dirty, trifling b*tch she would turn out to be. That was my first love—every element of the streets.

I was kicking it with Leon Jordan, Alhan Phillips, James Hampton, Orson Robinson, Nigel Collins, Pimpin' Bob, Talton Robinson, Hardrock, Tyrone (Ronnie) Jackson, Shy, and Bobo's younger brother.

Wall Street was still poppin'. I was still a frequent visitor to the Mad Pad, a regular—damn near a resident. I was fuckin' on Derek Brown's sister, Stephanie Richardson.

Christmas on Wall Street was crazy that year. That day, it was so many of us on the block—a very large gathering of our village. Earlier that day, me and G.P. had pushed over to Wall Street to buy some gold weed. The streets were slippery because of the mist and light rain that morning, and we fell on the moped.

I was on the back, holding four quarts of Old English 800 malt liquor we had just copped from Checkmate Market. But I saved the drank. That evening on Wall Street, there were about three knock-down, drag-out fights. I was out there with them cats, drinking 12-year-old scotch and snorting powder, kicking it with my folks. Stan had the video camera out on the porch, mounted on a tripod, capturing all the action.

Of course, with all the drinking—and this being Oak Park—there was bound to be a squabble or two. Walter Anderson and Michael Smith, respectively. Then New Boy and Mike got down in the street—old-school style. Just hands. No guns. No other weapons. It was all love—no malice afterward. Just some dysfunctional family shit—the kind of thing that happens in all urban communities.

I had been kicking it hard all morning with G.P. on 4th Ave. Smoking bomb-ass gold weed—the kind of weed that had thick, sticky resin coming out the back of the joint when you blew it. Fire ass weed. No bullshit bammer weed. That old-school gold weed came budded up, but it still had seeds—and it was very strong. You could not hit that shit hard without choking immediately.

G.P. had pushed all the way from The Heights to Mrs. Usher's house just to fuck with us on 4th Ave. for Christmas. We had a good-ass time. This would be the last time I would see Conrad. My last Christmas with blood. He was killed while I was in juvenile hall—only 14 years old. Shot in the head on 11th Ave., off MLK Boulevard, by this fool named Dennie Spain.

My mother came to visit me that Sunday out on Keifer Boulevard and gave me the sobering news about my bro. I was crushed, to say the least. Conrad was my dog. My brother. My friend. At the time, I was in H Unit—me and Hardrock. Carl Webb was in C Unit. We had Oak Park niggas in every unit.

We were all waiting for this fool to land in any of our units. But fortunately for me—he came to my unit. Where me and Hardrock were eagerly waiting to get in that ass. This was H Unit—a housing unit for the worst actors. Management problems. Kid murderers. YA babies. All that bad-acting shit. Fools being tried as adults.

So we waited up all night for the staff to bring that boy to our unit. Me and Hardrock could see each other from our room windows—we were right across the hall from each other. We knew—without having to say a word—that we were going to bang blood at breakfast. So, as the game would have it, we stomped him out. Knocked the boy's grill out. Got in that ass—until the staff pulled us off him. That move got me sent to Boys Ranch.

Me, Hardrock, Carl Webb, Mario Keola, and Tyrone Johnson— we were all there together. All young hitters. I ended up getting sent to CYA—for some weed I got caught with at The Ranch. But I would be home the next year, ready to make my bones in the game. A young wig-splitta.

I was sent to California Youth Authority—a juvenile prison of sorts. The place California sent its incorrigibles. The fuck-ups from all over the state. Mostly Black and Brown youth—because we have it the worst in the courtrooms across California. I was already over six feet tall. I had the unfortunate timing of failing the Boys Ranch program—all because of a little bit of weed I had hidden in the cast on my sprained ankle. I had hurt my ankle playing basketball in the gym at night. And for that, they sent me to CYA.

Being Black and male is enough to get sent to Death Row in Amerikkka—without even committing a crime. And I just had some weed. This is how all young men and boys of color are treated in this nation's court system. While I was in there, I met brothers from all over California. I was tall—about 6'4" by then. Skinny, wiry, and mannish as hell. A real live Oak Park nigga. A live wire.

I wasn't able to be housed with men my own age—I was taking advantage of them. I was very aggressive. Very violent. And I loved to squabble. I was one of the few cats my age who had females coming to visit them. My mother would bring young, fast-ass girls to me. So it was good. I was about whatever.

I had spent my childhood in a wild hood, so there was hardly anything I hadn't already seen, heard of, or participated in. This was just another level. Part and parcel of the game. A temporary setback for a major comeback. I was already banging this OP shit. So I just had fun until they decided where they were going to send me.

CHAPTER THIRTEEN

I was repping my region of Cali, my city, and my hood to the fullest extent possible. While locked up, I met cats from Oakland, just 70 miles from Sacramento. One would become a great friend of mine in later years—James Holloway, from West Oakland, Ghost Town, to be exact, aka Holly Rock. Back then, he was a little cat, about 5'2, but solid. We were locked up together at O.H. Close in Stockton, CA, after I was transferred from NRCC Reception Center.

Eventually, I got too big for O.H. Close and was sent to Y.T.S.—down by LA in Ontario, CA. While there, I met Monster Kody from Eight Trey Gangsters, along with Treetop from Bounty Hunter Bloods out of Watts, Mosko, Big Loaf, and a few other Hunta's. From Y.T.S., I was sent to Preston, and finally, I paroled.

When I came home, I was 6'4, 195 pounds—looking like a grown-ass man. But the truth was, I had already looked like a grown man before my capture and incarceration. I had been buying alcohol, playing with guns, robbing shit, taking shit—involved in every aspect of the game.

I was Oak Park, bred and reared in the streets. In my environment, violence was like oxygen—it was everywhere.

Back on the turf, 4th Avenue became my daily stomping grounds. I was running with Eric Connerly, Nigel Collins (aka Big Insane), Shawn (Demon) Collins, Orson Robinson, Pimpin' Bob, Charlie B. (Bonton), Carl Murphy, and Talton Robinson. This was Pebble Beach— named by Shawn Collins, and known for Coke water (Sherm/PCP) and marijuana—all sold separately. I was one of the original members of this round table.

This was the birthplace of NHYB (Neighborhood Young Bloods) and NHP (Neighborhood Piru). Both fell under the 456 acronym. I am the one who started the Neighborhood Pirus in honor of 4th Avenue Park's first title—Neighborhood Park.

Nigel Collins was the creator of the Neighborhood Young Bloods, also located in this hallowed place. So, Oak Park Neighborhood Young Bloods and Oak Park Neighborhood Pirus are all-inclusive of 456—all from the same family tree. Both came to life on 4th Avenue.

4th Avenue was also home to The Mob due to Shawn Collins' presence and base of operations being right there. The Mob was also posted at Oak Park Market and 5th Avenue. This crew consisted of Doug Wayne Erwin, Base Pipe Mike, Pete Brown, Tony Ellis, and Randy Moses, who got put on later.

The Mob was formed because my big homies linked up with the 69 Mob from 69 Village in East Oakland, CA. Big Rudy Henderson was the brains behind the diplomatic and political ties between Oak Park and this East Bay Mob movement.

We were importing hitters from my hood under contract—for heavy demolition work or construction work. As needed. Whatever it was about, we were about that work. There was a war going on at this time in Oakland, around '81, '82, '83. It was really smacking. And I was ten toes down—in the dirt.

We were the only niggas banging the city—had been for years. At that time, there were no Crips in Sacramento. We were—and still are— the largest and most dominant street organization in Sacramento. We were the originals—the first of the Blood/Piru movement in Sacramento city proper. It was us, the young niggas back then, that laid the foundation and set the tone for this thing of ours to grow and blossom.

We set the trend, those of my generation. We were pushing this DAMU street tribe in the city. I was there from the beginning. I am an original founder. An original Neighborhood Piru. Not many people know the original meaning of the word Blood as it pertains to Black people. It was originally an acronym:

Brotherly **L**ove **O**verriding **O**ppression and **D**estruction. Just like **CRIP** stood for:

Community **R**evolution **I**n **P**rogress.

And Young Bloods represented the young brothers who went to Vietnam to fight for some bullshit. The term Blood was also meant to signify that we were all of one blood. And in my hood, the word Blood was always used as a term of endearment throughout my formative years.

CHAPTER FOURTEEN

⟨ ⟩

When Nigel was moving and shaking up shit in the city, banging hard and giving it to the Crips in the South Area, I was already in prison, repping this 456 Neighborhood Piru gang.

The originals from this time on 4th Ave. were as follows: myself, Talton, Orson, Pimpin' Bob, Nigel Collins, and Eric Conerly. That was the nucleus—until Carl Webb, Hardrock, Peg, Badmouth, and other niggas got home from captivity.

I can recall in '82, Big Walt told Talton to tuck his red flag on Wall Street because they were over there taking James Hampton's tennis shoes off him. At the time, I was still in captivity, but I had called home and was told the news.

Wall Street was Funk Lord headquarters, and only blue and black flags were flown on Funk Lord turf. Even though 456 was what was being pushed, and we were connected to Pomona, CA Blood gang-wise through Nigel, who had begun his banging career in Pomona, in the Bar Jug and Islands community, 456 also represented Oak Park's phone number prefix.

At one time, all phone numbers in Oak Park began with the 456 prefix, and we pushed it—still do. We have strong roots in Pomona, CA because we have family from The P that emigrated down there, and Nigel lived in the Bar Jug community of Pomona.

This is where our PCP came from in the '70s and '80s. Fast Mackin' Dave and Lil' Brim used to come to Sac every summer. Their family, The Mob, was doing its business, smacking shit, wrecking shop—and that would be putting it mildly.

I recall vividly—the decibel of violence was at an all-time high. At least 10 bodies were dropped in succession, and this continued into the winter coming out of the summer. The winters were hot, and the summers were cold.

Every assignment was completed, and once completed, there were no mistakes or missed targets. I had skipped high school and went directly to the pros—the big leagues. This was not a joke. This thing of ours was cold-blooded logic at its core. My mentors were pushing a line that suckas dared not cross. And if a line was crossed, justice was swift. Street justice.

For violations. Them boys in the hood were mobbing hard. Pete Brown had just wrapped his two-toned green Deuce and a Quarter—aka Buick Electra 225. He had got that when he got out of YA for the murder he caught as a juvenile—just around the block from my house. Not long after, he flipped another one, coke white, brains blew, sitting on Zenith's and Vogues.

Randy Moses had a Lincoln Mark IV, clean as the board of health, and a clean-ass Cadillac Sedan DeVille, black and gray. Fat Dave was eating, too—having his paper right. Had a clean Buick Wildcat, dookie brown.

At a house party at the apartments on 4th Ave., me and Talton took all his music out of his car. Shawn made us return his property. I was constantly imposing my will upon Dave, among many others. He was 7-8 years older than I was at the time.

I was 15 years old—and had niggas twice my age scared to death to be around me and my dog Talton. I used to terrorize Dave's b*tchass.

64

We used to have him spooked at night on 5th Ave., in the alley, and he would go cry to Doug Wayne or Shawn. And Shawn would tell us to leave him alone.

I remember one night at the club, I snatched this nigga's shirt off him, fucking with his breasts—he was with Randy Moses. Me and Talton were animals in them streets. Real live justice servers.

CHAPTER FIFTEEN

The Mob was extorting Fat Dave and a few other cats who wanted to keep breathing while hustling. You could hustle—if you paid the Mob. If Dave wasn't paying or serving some type of purpose monetarily, Shawn would have released the hounds on him, and that would have been very ugly.

These young boys were about that life—stomp-down killers. Murder was business, and these niggas were all about handling business.

We were getting our PCP by the gallon from Southern California— Pomona, to be exact. It had been many moons back when catching a flight was still good to move product.

You didn't even need an ID to catch a flight back then.

Just a ticket and a name.

We would carry sealed glass 7UP bottles, just walk on the plane, and be back in Sac in 45 minutes.

It was only an up-and-down plane ride.

We would use a funnel to transfer the work into one-ounce bottles of vanilla extract, then cut the product with motor starting fluid. Straight poison for your brain. At the same time, powder coke was being pumped, and high-grade marijuana was moving as well.

Back then, myself and Talton were 4th Ave enforcers—little wild-ass niggas you did not want to fuck with. We looked to destroy someone every day. We were terrible actors. Every weekend on Stockton Blvd., we were knocking someone out, stripping them naked, taking their money and any other valuables they had on them.

We were beating fools down mercilessly—ambulances were hauling niggas out the clubs on stretchers. Shawn feared we would eventually beat someone to death. It got to the point where he just stopped taking us to the clubs. We were not predictable. We were not controllable.

We would say we were going to act civilized, but as soon as someone was outta pocket—We were on that ass. Dragging shit. Especially if someone acted as if they were not aware of their surroundings and location—It went bad fast. This was Oak Park—and, therefore, our universe. Our world. And if you were not a member of this Oak Park family, you were automatically an enemy of the Oak Park state. 4th Avenue, in particular.

The Mob was also pushing hop at the Big Park. There was a well-oiled machine running daily—good money was made every single day. Another operation was being run at Springer's Liquor Store. The Mob was mobbed up with Felix Mitchell from Oakland, CA—The 69 Mob, to be exact. It was favor for a favor back then, and they were moving that work.

Big work was pumping from these two locales, respectively. My brothers from another mother, Shawn D. Collins, and Nigel O. Collins, had a mother named Merlene—may Allah rest her soul—who ran a barbecue joint up at Springer's Liquor Store. Stephanie's Take-Out was the name of the spot. It was a little walk-up joint where you would step into a small vestibule, order your plate, and take your food to go. No seats, no fancy setup—just real Oak Park hood shit. The food was good. I didn't eat pork or shellfish, but I did partake in the beef ribs and a few other things on the menu.

Merlene's daughters, Stephanie and Mimi, would be in the kitchen often—that's what we called it—the kitchen. Tanya Brown too, another sister to them, and a sister to me as well. I would later be involved in a major gunfight right in front of the kitchen, on the side of Springer's, in the summer of that year.

And the crazy part? It was over some pussy that belonged to neither of the gunfighters. The participants of the shootout had no ownership, no claim, no stake in the coochie. But that's the game. That's part of it.

Greg Murphy got shot in the back—standing right next to me. I was busting my hammer in the middle of the street, and Shawn was busting his .44 off the porch—right above and behind me. I was 15 years old—which is grown in the hood. The nigga I was busting back at was twice my age.

And to this day, you can get your birthday taken in Oak Park over some pussy or a female that has no affiliation with you. We play that shit heavy. And most of the time? Truth be told, the b*tch ain't shit.

The night of the fireworks at Springer's, I had pushed over to Gary Goethe's joint across the street from Talton's crib on 4th and 24th St. and grabbed some shells for my hammer, which I had already unloaded earlier in the day—dumping that thang at the fools who were shooting at us.

Later that night, on my way home to 36th, after picking up my female from 1st Ave., my sister Felicia and my girl Shante Rai were pushing in Felicia's black Ford Pinto—the car she had gotten for her 16th birthday a few months earlier.

We were rolling down Sacramento Blvd. (now MLK Blvd.), making a right on 9th Ave., when we pulled up right next to Tim Prince in his canary yellow Deuce and a Quarter Buick.

I had spotted his car while we were coming up on 9th Ave. and timed it just right so that as we turned the corner, we were side by side.

I told Felicia to pick up speed—and as soon as we were lined up, I got to busting my gun through the driver's side window at Tim. I emptied my clip. All nine shots went straight through the sunroof of my sister's car.

My uncle Puddin had just cut that sunroof in our driveway—and that shit came in handy. It had been Tim's brother, Clint, who had busted on us up at Springer's earlier in the day. I caught them slippin' while turning. I think Clint was in the car too.

Shortly after this, I would become the first of my generation to be sent to the penitentiary. I saw a lot of things growing up—especially when it came to race and race relations.

But I had KOS—Knowledge of Self. I had been enlightened by the Nation of Islam. I was told at Shabazz's Fish and Chips—located on 35th St.—that the Black man is God and the original man on this earth. This was told to me by a couple of brothers who would later become my enlighteners—both at that time and in later years. Big Winfred Smith—may peace be on that brother. John Usher—may peace be on that brother, too.

And another brother—Jabbar—who used to walk around the hood carrying a huge-ass verb stick. They taught me to go for self—that the Black man must be the God of himself. I had already known the South African proverb, "First, they had the Bible, and we had the land. Now we have the Bible, and they have the land."

But as a man-child, I had yet to shed my negative ways in this so-called Promised Land. I had betrayed myself. I had slipped into savagery.

CHAPTER SIXTEEN

*The willingness to change strategy is a fundamental
requirement of intelligent community engaged in
a protracted struggle against an enemy.*

- Manu Ampin.

Racial oppression is predominantly exercised through economic discrimination, judicial bias, and political inefficiency. This often contributes to the manifestation of an obfuscated identity crisis and, in many cases, leads to subtle self-hatred. Consequently, things like law, education, and social responsibility—taking care of family and community or earning a living legitimately—became, based on my attitude, ways, words, and actions, things I rejected outright.

I didn't just reject them—I was diametrically opposed to them. Opposed to what, you might ask? Everything. Ironically, the very attitude that formed the foundation of my identity as a nigga didn't protect me, empower me or shield me in any way from the devil's civilization.

It didn't protect me politically. It didn't protect me economically. It didn't protect me socially. Instead, it exposed me—and prepared me—for a judicial apparatus that, according to the 13th Amendment to the Constitution, would literally re-enslave me. Not only that, but it kept me entrenched in criminal activity that was destructive—to my family, my community, and other misguided, misdirected, lost, mentally deaf, mentally dumb, mentally blind brothers like myself.

The young and marginalized often mistakenly respond to discriminatory and biased policies by engaging in crime or assuming the role of "niggas"—not realizing that we are not only politically ineffective but, as a consequence, we voluntarily surrender ourselves over to a system that was designed from its very inception to destroy us as a people. And worse?

It uses our own ignorance to grind us into social fertilizer—nourishing the seeds of the next generation in order to continue producing expendable bodies to feed this political beast and keep its financial belly full.

I once interpreted incarceration as nothing more than a byproduct of my skin color. It would take me almost a decade from when I first entered prison to realize that changing the trajectory of my self-destructive behavior—on my own terms—would have to happen with or without the ineffective assistance of the *prisoncrats*.

This realization would become an offensive affront to the CDCR (California Department of Corrections and Rehabilitation)—which is really just a Department of Needs. And this offense would subtly put me in the crosshairs—not just of the devils who keep me hostage but of some recreant prisoners as well.

A Cognitive Emergence

When I entered the state prison system for the first time in the early '80s at the tender age of 16, I was already a man-child. A father, with a baby mama, a side piece, and another side piece to complement the first one—just in case one lost their way.

The social landscape was entirely different from what exists today. Because of my experiences with the game and street violence, I entered prison with a warrior-like mentality. More of a prisoner of politics than a political prisoner—with the utmost respect to those who are held hostage today for acts predicated upon politically conscious ideology.

I was the first of my peers to enter prison and the first Sacramento/ Oak Park Damu (Blood) to enter prison from the Sacramento Valley, area code 916. Those of my generation—within my social circle—came to prison from neighborhoods and community conditions that were poised to murder us in a myriad of ways. And bullet wounds and scars— not tattoos—were our chevrons to show our combat service in the game that is not a game.

We were young Black men, full of angst—but we were also signifying an urban environmental Black message to other and older prisoners that we were warriors.

We were evolving from boyhood. We were young men in rebellion, living on the coattails of arrested development, having grappled and wrestled with the abuses and elements of poverty, surviving violent incidents, and struggling to respect those in leadership positions— especially when they demonstrated more caricature than character.

Back in the '80s, I was familiar with quite a few individuals I ran into in the pen—cats who had reputations in the free world as notorious stomp-down killers, gangstas, and, in some cases, dope fiends— sometimes a combination of both.

But now? Now, they were masquerading as revolutionary erudites with criminally predatory mentalities. Their revolutionary efforts were more nugatory than effective. And I would discover, decades later, that these efforts amounted to nothing more than ornamental sentiments— words and gestures that attracted the prison investigative security squads, who began targeting entire generations or sectors of sincerely conscious prisoners for removal from CDCR mainlines.

This led to a dramatic deterioration of social awareness and respect among California prisoners as a whole. Like a lot of young men who come to prison, I was searching for an identity. Looking for structure.

Some of the reading materials I encountered upon entering prison were radical and revolutionary.

This information provided me with a sense of pride because I identified with those who had confronted bigoted devils and fought back against the forces of evil and racism. I was introduced to the philosophies and ideologies of some of the most brilliant African thinkers.

I read politically charged literature about the Black Panther Party for Self-Defense—who I was already familiar with as a child growing up in Oak Park. I studied the BLA (Black Liberation Army), the PRGA (Provisional Government of the Republic of New Afrika), RAM (Revolutionary Action Movement), NAPO (New Afrikan People's Organization), AM31st (Amistad 31st), the NOI (Nation of Islam), the Moorish Science Temple, the Knights of Liberty, and the African Blood Brotherhood—just to name a few.

I did not see these groups and community action organizations as gangs or criminal enterprises, as the United States government tried to portray them. Instead, I saw them as freedom fighters. Unsung heroes. Heroes in the canon of Black history—or as we call it, our story. Our New Afrikan history.

But the way I was internalizing this material at this tender age did not lead me to a higher understanding. Instead, it deepened my rage. The rage that fueled my hostility toward the nation-state's complicit racism reinforced my sense that I was only a victim. And that mentality? It allowed me to justify my criminal actions. It compounded a host of social problems that only served to continue the elimination—through incarceration—of society's undesirables.

I would learn that as much as I strove to develop my physical strength, it would be my mental strength that would get me over the hump of mental death. My big homie Ice Water—Big Dirty Earn's older brother—would emphasize learning and reading about my ancestors and the conditions of our communities worldwide. He taught me that knowledge was just as powerful as lifting weights and doing burpees.

I was never conscious of the fact that the tensely strained bow of oppression ultimately takes revolutionary aim at the power of the oppressor. Instead, I continued my education—but not in the right way. I was becoming more of a predator in my own community. And later in this narrative, this street-to-prison correlation will become even clearer.

Over 30+ years ago, those of my generation who ended up in prison came in during the Ronald Reagan crack pandemic—the same one that swept through the Sacramento Valley and the surrounding Bay Area like the flu.

One of my close childhood friends, A.C.—aka Anthony Cannon— would become the first millionaire of my peer group. And one of the best to ever do it. And not get a life sentence for hustling in the United Snakes of America.

What people outside the urban centers and ghettos of this nation don't understand is that hustlers hustle out of desperation. They ain't doing this shit to look good or be cute. They're getting down to feed their families.

To feed themselves. To help those they love. And love? Love is the most powerful force in the universe. Period.

We live and die and are reinvented because of love. In this era, the tale of Too Short, Ice-T, Eric B. and Rakim, and Whodini—who personally visited my community as guests of my relative Pat Shaver during the height of the crack era—was our soundtrack.

Most of the music that came out of Northern California chronicled what it was really like to be a youngster from our communities— navigating the perils of poverty, pain, paper-chasing, prison, and street tribal warfare. Some of Oak Park's hip-hop artists told the same story. Cats like Bad Mouth and Homicide—both of whom are my homies and Oak Park citizens

We did not possess a political agenda against the powers that be, nor did we have a revolutionary ideology or even a collective criminal strategy. Our primary goal was to get out of prison alive and intact, but until that time came, we were determined to keep our chin up, chest out, and boots laced tight in order to secure ourselves in situations where prison cats not only failed to protect us but typically left it up to prisoners to fend for themselves.

At the time, we had yet to crystallize an understanding of how capitalism is the driving force behind classism and how classism is the principal impetus of competition, fueling crime, violence, and other components of social division that we experienced firsthand in our own communities. What we did understand was this:

We were Black. We were from Sacramento. We were Bloods/Pirus. And we were behind enemy lines. In these wars in California, most of the residents of Sac and the Bay Area were heavily outnumbered, so cohesion became our basic focus.

One of my big homies at this time was Bahye', who developed the 916 collective in DVI, Tracy—at the time known as Gladiator School. This was around '83, "84—the same place I landed at the age of 16.

A father already, I had a couple of females on my line, running. A couple of white girls, plus Shanie, my twin boys' mother, Donille, and Sandy Dawson—the latter, a white girl from Rancho Cordova, the white-girl haven of eastern Sacramento, CA.

Shanie's big-headed ass was visiting me back then. I was also in Tracy with my uncle JB and relative John Earl—and Troy Allen from the Bay, who had moved to Oak Park. I hadn't seen Troy since they hit the jewelry store lick in '81.

I had just come to Tracy the previous summer to visit my brother Lil' James, my relly Detchie, John Earl, and my uncle JB—before I myself was enslaved in the same slave camp.

By then, Detchie had just left for Solano, which had just been built, and James had just gone to Susanville. I was a man-child—large and mature for my years.

I was 6'4, 190-195 pounds—slim and cocky as a motherfucker. I stood on my own two and rocked out with my cock out. I let my shit hang—and I was about that life. Period.

I had a very large number of community residents in Tracy—a gang of homies and a gang of cats from Sacramento in general.

A lot of my homies who were there from my hood were members of the infamous tribe—founded at this same institution in the late '60s due to observing the rivalry between LA-based street tribes—mostly Bloods and Crips.

At this time, these street tribes were predominantly LA-based and at war with each other. I had just arrived at the institution a week after a Crip had been killed by a Blood in the Field House—a gym inside the prison.

So violence was a very real reality—a constant. Weaker cats were getting raped and having their shit taken. If you were a b*tch—or had b*tchin you—someone would bring it out pretty quick.

A new ethos had serendipitously evolved—an attitude that distinguished the social structure inside the prison, ensuring that divisive dynamics and outside entities didn't establish themselves within our collective unity.

It wouldn't be long before Crips from Sacramento started entering the system. And because of certain Oak Park dignitaries, they would not be allowed to walk certain mainlines in and around the system—due to our communities being divided by color lines.

The red and blue lines, of course. We fell into a murderous rivalry— one that continues to this day. While in Tracy, I was educated by a few of my big homies. I witnessed several up-close, personal, brutal murders— and countless stabbings.

All of my big folks who were there with me were BGF (Black Guerrilla Family). So were a lot of the big folks from Del Paso Heights (DPH). I was the only Damu from Sac in the pen at that time—at least from my peer group. I met a Damu from Lincoln Park Syndicate Mob named Cle Bone.

I had a partner who had just come to Tracy from YA—someone I had been in juvenile hall with—named Roy Gordon. He was a BGD—a Black Gangster Disciple—before they dropped "Black" from the first name.

He was from Chicago. My older mentors—being up under that Black Revolutionary Act—were educating all the Bloods who came through Tracy. These brothers weren't just educating Bloods, though. They were educating non-affiliates, too.

We Bloods were short in numbers—but we were all about that action, so we were widely respected. And me? I loved being the underdog. Loved being doubted. Loved being underestimated. Tracy was a very violent place at this time.

It had just been featured in TIME Magazine as the second most dangerous prison in the United States. Only Angola Penitentiary was ranked worse. There were constant assaults, robberies, and rapes. All of that shit was happening at the same time. This shit was no joke. You kept your poker face on. And when the time came—You did not hesitate to swing that iron.

As it would happen, Sacramento as a whole was hella deep at Tracy—mostly Oak Park and DPH—and we were united. My homies—Bora, Shabazz, J. Mack, King, Ice Water, my relly John Earl, Coop, Bahye'—were all stomp-down hitters. At Tracy, I learned to make weapons and, more importantly, how to use them. And I did use them—on a couple of occasions.

There were no guns in these housing units, so when shit popped off and got real funky, the C/O's would just shoot gas and slam the gates in the hallways. And shit got funky daily. Several times a day, I would run wild through Tracy—becoming incorrigible. We were all in D-Wing, in the day room, and we carved a big "916" into the day room wall.

Hank Ford was there, and so was Derek Franklin—both from Sac—DPH and The Gardens, respectively. It was so live in D-Wing that at night, during day room, the staff would unlock the day room door—and huge clouds of weed smoke would waft up out of the day room and hit the C/O in the face.

And the officer? He would mind his goddamn business. This was a different day and time. CO's stayed out of a motherfucker's business. Not like now, where they got a gun on you in most levels above two.

Back then, you could actually do your thing in Tracy—and not stress about the rollers getting in your business. I had weekend visits lined up and night visits, too. I was velvet with it, stayin' laced and gettin' shown real love in the visiting room.

Sandy—the white girl—who was older than me by a couple of years, would push up there at night. And Red and Shanie would come with my mother. This activity continued until I was transferred to Folsom State Prison—at 17 years old. I would turn 18 in Folsom's SHU.

I was sent there for being a young cat who wasn't following the rules. I was also involved in some violent situations—and participated in cadences with my folks, which was not allowed per CDC policy (and still isn't to this day).

We had been observing and celebrating Black August (Weusi Agosto). A lot of Afrikans marching in military formation was upsetting to the powers that be—to say the least. We were several hundred deep at this time—shouting so loud that the yard was overcome by our voices. We were commemorating the lives lost on the battlefields of the wilderness of North America.

We had been dying at the hands of our oppressors since arriving on the shores in 1619—kidnapped, of course. I would be the youngest cat in Folsom—until another young cat came in: Lil' Bill from Grape Street.

I was close to a couple of Crip boys I met while attending the hidden university that is prison—if you're doing the time and not letting the time do you. Dave from Harlem. J. Stone from 60s.

Me and J. Stone would become very close friends in this environment. I had come to Folsom smack-dab in the middle of a war between the Mexican Mafia and the BGF (Black Guerrilla Family).

I was released from the hole once the peace treaty was called and agreed to by all parties. This was 1985. The cat who called the peace treaty was killed by his own folks a year later in Tehachapi SHU. 1985 would be the most violent year in Old Folsom prison history.

It was a murderous year—at least 360-370 stabbings and 14 to 20 homicides. And no lockdowns. The shit was on the news daily. This was a dungeon of a prison—over 100 years old at the time. Maybe two or three people were charged with murder. Some pleaded guilty to manslaughter.

The ones in charge just didn't care—as long as the violent acts were not racially motivated or involved the staff, they just didn't care. So, stabbings were commonplace. And you could wear your flag colors. So red and blue flags were flying proudly and loudly. You were allowed to take gang-related photos—All that self-admission shit the C/O's like you to take so that they can identify a motherfucker and document membership rolls.

When the peace treaty was called, every one of us was let out the hole at the same time—And pandemonium ensued, to say the least. Because of the media attention in Sacramento involving all the racial violence, the prison was under scrutiny. So, to stop the violence racially, a deal was made—And as long as there was no racial violence, we had carte blanche to do whatever. Which is why that year was outlandishly violent.

CHAPTER SEVENTEEN

There were many senseless killings and stabbings, of course. But me? Being an Oak Park nigga—I survived and thrived. My folks were doing the same. Fat Kev, Kevin Chaney, Pimpin' Bob, Big Virgel, Terrill Robinson, Earnest Tribit, his lil' bro Trib, Nigel, Shawn Collins—all these boys were scrambling, getting their chips and handling business. D. Woods, Bad Mouth, Young Mays, Nunu, Big Virge—they had the Mob knockin' hard. The hood was live, and paper was moving everywhere—block to block, corner to corner.

On my first day back in the hood, I was with my relly—Flashlight Chaney, Talton, Terrill, Terauchi, Kenya, Markern, Mays, Fat Kev, Huey Robinson. A whole squad of us pushed up to Florin Mall in the South area, buying clothes, shoes, and shit. Mario Calhoun was there too—a very close lil' bro of mine. We made the trek downtown and did the same damn thing. Then we went back to the hood hit Anderson's Liquor Store to grab some more yak. I made it home around 3 AM—drunk and tree-high off that bomb-ass weed. I hadn't smoked in over a year, being in the SHU with Darnell Royston. Solitary confinement had my system clean so that first hit was a system shock for real.

So we were back. Who? The originals—myself, Nigel, and Talton, among a few others. And The Sacramento Bee reported that the recent release of several gang members back into the community had sparked a rash of homicides. We were out. Owners beware. We barred none and faded all. Busta's be wary. Suckas stay in the house. We were home. And the boogeyman was home, living, walking, breathing karma. And that man—was the god M.S. Allah.

While I had been kidnapped and confined against my will in the late '80s, some L.A. cats had infiltrated the city. They were sneaking in and out of my turf, unnoticed, unseen, and fucking with b*tches to sneak into the community and get a couple of dollars. Oak Park, size-wise, is fairly large and porous, so it was hard for us to seal off every entrance.

The first Bloods to come to Sac were OP/VN. As it would be, myself and Talton didn't want any outsiders in the community. So we were on that set-tripping shit. All day, every day. If you were not a resident—it was bad for you off top. No questions asked. All action. No fake pumping. Caught slipping? You were a victim of circumstance.

Nothing personal. This was all business. Family protecting family. We were trippin' on fools not from Sac in general after a while. So we made shit shake. We were body-snatching and head-bustin'. It was what it was. We got our smash on royally. It was a cold thing to be in The P— by the wrong ones—and not be from there!

While I was knocked in the game, stuck in the cage, my good friend G.P. had started to check major traps, getting hoe money and balling off that hard white shit. I had seen the boy on TV when the movie Colors came out in '88—the reporter was asking him if he banged. And G.P. tells the little white b*tchthat he banged about his money—that's all he was about. Money.

The nigga was fitted, in green from head to toe, and had his 5.0 drop-top Mustang sitting right behind him, squatted clean on them thangs (Dayton's and Vogues). That same year, he was knocked by the feds. This was my real patna, my A1 from day one. A good nigga, the kind that's rare in this day and age. The boy was the first cat his age to go federal.

81

He was smashing in the game, and squares were hatin'—like they always do—on a real playa. He was getting paper and had the bunnies hopping on that track for his scratch.

Right before he got knocked by the people, he had seen my little big-headed b*tchMarlo up at her job at AMPM Mini-Mart out on the south side of town. Since the little large-head b*tchwas looking like something to eat, he popped his game at her and dropped his book to see if she would bite.

She was pushing a '78 Seville, dookie brown but slightly clean. She had pictures of me in that thang and let him know she wasn't choosin'— she had a man. And his handle was Mark Sanders, from Oak Park.

"Do you know this nigga?" she asked. Of course, he replied. "That's my nigga."

Then he asked if she went to see me, and if so, did she get down for me? The answer was affirmative to both questions—and the nigga sent me some work to eat off of in the pen.

Back then, in CDC, you could have visits seven days a week. And I was getting visits every day, leaving to go to my job from visiting, while she was going to work. Folsom, being in Sacramento County, it was just a hop, skip, and a jump to get there.

And I stayed on the dance floor. The girl was running—had fresh track shoes on—running that thing across the line in the end zone every time. G.P., like a real nigga, shot her some cash too. This was—and still is—my brother from another mother, in a real way. He kept shit solid in Sac County Jail—but that's another story.

My patna Milk Dog had just got out—and got smacked (killed) on some bullshit out in the Heights. My other patna Wolf was smacked too—as soon as he got out in the Willow Trees in the Heights.

Niggas were getting smacked left and right—this was the '80s, the height of the crack pandemic. Milk Dog was an original Blood from DPH, along with—but not limited to—Leon Johnson aka Wooga, G.P.,

Darnell Royston, Chester Chambers, Raymond Pitts, and Kenny Pitts—all out them Plazas, a housing project in The Heights.

Anthony Perry and his brother Time Bomb were both original Sacramento Crips—same as their uncle, Rayford Nunley. We would fight these cats in the juvenile hall just because we thought they would be Crips.

Del Paso Heights also had a few Crip sets out there, but they weren't as active as the South Side Crips. The Heights also had a little clique of real hittas called The Dogs, based out of The Plazas. There was also a clique based out of The Gardens called The Dog Catchers. Donald Haily and a few other cats were pushing that Dog Catcher line.

I was cool with most of the Bloods collective—and eventually, they absorbed most, if not all, of The Dog Catchers and The Dogs out in The Heights. The first Crip set to emerge in Sac was the 29th Street Crips, based in South Sacramento, in the 29th Street Apartments.

The 24th Street Crips came later—just some Sacramento history for you. Before that, there weren't any Crips in South Sacramento. No Garden Blocc Crips—that would come later, when they would combine to survive. The Detroit BLD Bloods were the first Bloods in the south side of town, along with the Valley Hi Pirus, right in back of Meadowview. At that time, they weren't Bloods yet.

The Meadowview Bloods/Pirus emerged later. Most of these cats wanted to bang Oak Park—but as Oak Park gets down, we don't put niggas on or none of that L.A.-style shit. If you ain't from The P., you can't bang the set. Period.

Even with all this gang fuss, Sacramento is still 100% game-related—as well as gang-related. Niggas still pimp, hustle, grind, gamble—and will take heads for a slice of bread. And females? They get paper, too. They are just as dangerous and game-related as the niggas.

As with any species, especially human beings, the female species is the most vicious. You can see that in female lions—as well as in pit bulls.

But with humans—being at the top of the food chain—the females are the most conniving and analytical. They let you think it is what it is—when it ain't.

Malcolm X stated in his autobiography that he could never trust women. When asked why, his answer was:

"I seen them do too many foul things." I respect that—but you gotta trust your Queen over all the bullshit. Because Malcolm's wife, Betty, told him the cats weren't his friends—and he didn't listen. And that got him killed.

Sometimes—and more often than not—your woman can spot a b*tchmove in a man before you can. To see with your third eye—not just with your one-eyed monster. The females in my hood? They get paid—and they sock it to a nigga's pocket, as they should. I salute them all. Since we are close to the Bay Area, we share a lot of commonalities—that slick talk and game-related shit.

This is Northern California. And we get down this way. Fast game. Fast cars. And even faster women. But in Sac, Stockton, etc., you also have the gang element—and it is too entrenched to go anywhere. So, we have lines and boundaries.

And you will get your head busted playing in the city. And most definitely, you will get your shit busted playing in The Murder Mids. AKA Oak Park.

Having covered most of the things I wanted to share, it's time to get to my transformation. But before that, I will take the reader into the depth of my reinvention—my growth and development, my embrace of the knowledge of self, and my battle with fighting and killing the demons I have carried for years. I have stood tall and survived the bullshit because the fire within me burned hotter than the fire around me.

In these next few pages, I will share my wisdom with the reader—and try to bring some clarity and insight into some of the things most of us struggle with in this life. We look outside for the answers—never understanding that they are never found without. You were born with all the answers. Allah made it simple. People fuck it up—with ego, jealousy, envy, and hate.

I hope that with this narrative, I have shed light on the world we live in—as the first and original archetype of humanity, made in His image and likeness. And we should embrace our divinity.

But some of our people? They like being oppressed. So before you go to war with the devil over your people being in hell—make sure first that they don't like being there. Because some like it just fine. The darkness of ignorance suits them tailor-made.

CHAPTER EIGHTEEN

❧

This last chapter in my retrospective concerns change, reinvention, and having the foresight to see the big picture—to think outside the box, color outside the lines, and step out of your comfort zone.

What doesn't change—dies. A life that does not change is not a life worth living. A mind that does not change is dead. The only constant in our universe is change. It is happening right now—all around you. Life is about change. Period.

Allow me to share some words of wisdom in hopes that you see the world differently. Peace.

Investment towards liberation:

As I began to study and apply myself more fervently to the social dynamics in urban America, it became apparent that the same elements of oppression in society that produced the Bloods and Crips—as well as many other street organizations, gangs, and tribes from New York to California—were the same forces that produced us.

The same kind of homicide, fratricide, and patricide that was happening in one urban community was happening in all urban communities. The result? Nothing more, nothing less, than genocide.

Now, this violence occurs not only in urban hoods—but in rural hoods as well.

I was in and out of captivity throughout the '80s and '90s, and I began to notice the growing effects of what I call step-down oppression. They oppress us. We oppress each other in turn. And as a consequence, we prey on each other. That is pop psychology—a menticidal act, a phenomenon that rapidly spread throughout CDCR.

It would grow into what we have today: the rise of honor yards—also known as Enhanced Program Yards—villainous bastions that house so many alienated prisoners that the prison population has become completely polarized into opposing factions. One side accuses the other of being apostates, snitches, sellouts, and turncoats.

Meanwhile, prisoncrats manipulate this social dichotomy—a system they designed to keep the Security Housing Units (SHU) full. I was targeted for validation in 2008 while at Pelican Bay State Prison, accused of being a prison gang associate.

In 2011, I was validated as both a member of a movement from my hood and as a prison gang associate. The evidence used against me? A picture of George Jackson from the late '60s. A quote from a book he authored. A statement from a bottom-feeder inmate—a debriefer who pointed the finger at me.

A lying informant, claiming that I was a prison gang associate—which is an insidiously arbitrary accusation, considering that debriefed informants are not required to verify their information under penalty of perjury. These snitches can literally say whatever they want—with no accountability—and CDCR will take their word as law. Empirical evidence and qualitative research reveal something disturbing:

CDCR's management policies, as they exist in practice, are abusively exploitative—and are not primarily about security, safety, or violence containment. No more than political demagoguery sensationalizing crime is about public safety.

This system does nothing but milk taxpayers—fulfilling a bureaucratic financial demand to employ and expand an extremely huge workforce used to manage so-called dangerous prison gangs. And in the end, the hole and maximum-security housing units have become the primary interest.

The secondary interest—which in turn threatens the first—is to prevent the development of social consciousness and to stop prisoners from employing humane, peaceful strategies to liberate themselves from corrupt abuse. Abuses that run counter to penological interest. I want everyone to know that I am not a gang member of any kind.

But I am a servant of my People's liberation—from the chains of physical and psychological slavery. And I am an Oak Park community member—for life. The chains that trap our minds are real in this new era of Jim Crow. I continue to strive forward because, for one, I am impassioned with the knowledge that The Most High has my back. And that's something profound.

Significance can emerge from those of us who have been tossed into society's wastebasket of retribution. Besides—when it has come down to combat—I am undisputed in my 30+ combined years of confinement.

But suckas—with the help of correctional officers—have jumped me behind my back. If I were them, I would do the same thing—opposing someone like myself. But then again, me not being a coward—I never would. I have never betrayed another, including those who I know betrayed me. And that cuts deeper than any physical wound ever could.

I have recently written the Articles of Incorporation—with a mission statement—for O.P.G. (Our Progressive Growth). The purpose? To establish a 501(c)(3) nonprofit organization that could potentially play a role in reducing the violence in the Sacramento Valley area and surrounding communities.

My mission? To stall or stop the destruction of our young men and women—to keep them from entering the school-to-prison pipeline that is all too common in our communities nationwide.

I have invested a large amount of time in helping others decriminalize themselves—as well as myself. I have educated others during my confinement and slavery.

And as I said at the beginning of this retrospective, redemptive journey—I was exposed to the life-giving teachings of the 5% Nation of Gods and Earths (NGE) as a small child, right in the heart of Oak Park. And it came back full circle.

I had come back to my natural self—but while away from the free cipher (home). I had a long talk—with myself and God. "If you don't change your ways, these crackers are never going to let you go home." Everything in nature seeks balance—this is called homeostasis. I sought mine—especially after my youngest child, Imara, was incarcerated.

She was locked up for some bullshit—something that could've been handled in another way, form, or fashion. I had to get home—to her and to my family.

For years, I shied away from redemption—from my own redemption, I should say. I thought it was a sign of weakness to stop banging—to stop acting ignorant—to stop being violent and aggressive. I was worried about what others would think. After all—this was Mark Sanders. M.S. Mr. Manslaughta. Oak Park Mark. Would they think I was weak? That flashed up there—on my mental movie screen. And many of our youth? They have the same concerns. The same anxiety. But I know better now.

A sincere redemptive effort—to change yourself mentally—takes an enormous amount of courage and self-discipline. It takes arduous self-discipline to be reborn. A man must be the maker of himself—and making positive change in one's life is ultimately a sign of strength— never weakness. And I have never been a weak cat.

I have fought against shit all my life—just the wrong shit. Weakness is being afraid of the challenge to become a better you. I developed a focus—and I stuck to it. The strongest people on this earth are not the most protected—They are the ones that must strive and struggle—

against adversity, barriers, and obstacles—and surmount them to survive. Period.

I had chosen wisdom—to embrace my higher self, that God in me. The true and living—the self-created—in the image and likeness of The Most High, The Creator Himself.

To be a student—as well as a teacher. To strive for self-improvement all the time—not sometimes. To seek perfection on all facets of the square. I knew as a child that the depth of your knowledge determines the circumference of your activity. That's simple math. And Allah created the universe simple—man makes it hard. So, at this point, I had two choices:

I could do this time—or let it do me. I could serve the time—or make the time serve me. I don't have to tell you which one I chose. I knew that life is mathematics. God wrote the whole universe in mathematics.

The universe is written in the laws of mathematics—and our ancestors knew this. Almost all ancient and modern scientists have stated this in one form or another. Understanding these laws and living by them puts you in harmony with the grand scheme of things.

Until you do this, you are going against the grain—and on track to encounter problem after problem. Every system in the universe, no matter how big or small, is governed by the same laws. The same principles. And guess who is at the heart and center of it all? You. That's who. You are the question and the answer, all in one. It is all inside you.

The Atom—protons, neutrons, and electrons. The Black Universe Family—Man, Woman, and Child. The Solar System—Sun, Moon, and Stars. Look up the 42 Declarations of Ma'at. That is us. We wrote that. We wrote it thousands of years before the Bible—long before the devil tricked you out of your natural mind and self.

I went back to the 5%—but I really never left. I was just using the knowledge for negativity. I knew the 120-degree lessons—but I wasn't standing on my square like I should have been. However—I am a Titan. A God Cipher Divine Culture—Not a novice. Not an adept.

90

At this point in my life—in my living Quran—I had to embrace the truth. That it is all on me. The man in the mirror. That it all begins—and ends—with me. I blame myself for any failings in my life—just as I credit myself for all the accents in my life.

And I vow to exhibit right conduct, to be right-thinking, and to move right and exact in all my undertakings. From this point on, in my cipher, I acknowledge that I have participated in the destruction of my community—As well as myself. And my family. By not being there for the babies—when I should have been.

I have rivers of blood on my hands. I have spent decades in hell. But my mental was never trapped—or otherwise chained up. Because I never stopped striving. I never stopped seeking. I never stopped learning, growing, changing. Growth and development are lifelong—And knowledge is the foundation of everything in the universe.

We are taught in the lessons—That anything that is 100% weak and wicked is the devil—Regardless of the color of their skin. I was always mindful of this fact.

So, I never sank to that level—Not even during my fall from grace, not even during my search for redemption. Thankfully—I was pretty close, though.

Wisdom is the Way

Wisdom (noun):

1. The effectual mediating principle or personification of God's will in the creation of the world.

2. a. (1) Accumulated information—philosophic or scientific learning. (2) Accumulated lore or instinctive adaptation of learning: the ability to discern inner qualities and essential relationships.

3. a. An embodiment of wisdom: a wise attitude or course of action. b. A person of superior intellectual attainments.

4. The teaching of ancient wise men (as of Babylon, Egypt, or Palestine), relating to the art of living and sometimes to philosophical problems concerning the universe, man, or God—forming a class of literature represented in the Hebrew books of **Job, Proverbs, Ecclesiastes, Ecclesiasticus**, and **The Wisdom of Solomon**.

Webster's Dictionary, Third New Edition (International).

Lao Tzu said, "The journey of a thousand miles begins with one step."

Every man and every woman who has reached the age of discernment should be seeking the 12 jewels—jewels for life. These are:

Knowledge, Wisdom, Understanding, Freedom, Justice, Equality, Food, Clothing, Shelter, Peace, Love, and Happiness.

All of us, having the ability to think in pragmatic terms, should seek these jewels in our daily lives. To achieve liberty and fulfillment—to obtain the things we need and the things we want in life—we must seek our higher selves.

We must seek within and without. But seeking within is most critical. Your mind is the master—we are the sum total of all of our thoughts. You are what you think—as well as what you eat.

In the Supreme Mathematics, Knowledge is 1: the foundation of all things in existence. Wisdom is 2: the manifestation of that knowledge—it is knowledge in action.

Man-is-festation. Man-fest—speak, act—action is wisdom. It is the separation that brings about the beginning of life. It is that huge Big Bang—the creation of the universe. It is the formation of every single-celled organism, which multiplies from a single life.

It is the partition God renders when He emphatically states, "Let there be light,"—separating light from dark matter. The light from the dark. The sky from the ocean. The heavens from the earth. The separation of man from his rib to create woman.

Wisdom is the woman—it is the womb one traverses to become mentally born. Knowledge and Wisdom give birth to Understanding—just as Man and Woman give birth to the Child. Wisdom is the work—it is the way to make knowledge known.

"In the beginning was the Word, and the Word was with God, and the Word became flesh." God's Knowledge was made manifest (born) through words—to create life.

Wisdom is the reflection in time—Knowledge is static and timeless. It is the stillness before the Big Bang—The explosion brings Understanding through the 4th dimension—which is Time.

Wisdom is water. It was the Great Flood that drowned the evil and wicked in the biblical era of Noah. It was the ocean that drowned Pharaoh's army when Moses parted the Red Sea. It is the Universal Solvent—in which all things dissolve in Allah's good time.

I am very well-read—I read voraciously. Thinking constructively is an exercise for the brain. I am constantly head-bent—reading, learning, growing, and changing. As well as conditioning myself through constant training. One only learns what one teaches oneself.

If you have ever stood on the shores of Lake Tahoe, in the mountains of Northern California—or stood at the precipice of the Grand Canyon—or just stood by the ocean shore at night in silence, feeling that connection, that vast, infinite presence within your being—then you have felt "It." What the Taoists call Oneness. What the Muslims call Allah. What most call God. That is what I felt growing up in Oak Park—walking through the Big Park at night, alone. Only—it was a tiny bit dimmer. But it was there.

Allah's truth is within us all—it is always there. From before we are born—it is just a seed, waiting patiently for the light to bring it to life. Wisdom is that bright light. In the Book of Proverbs (King James

Version), Solomon the King chooses Wisdom over all the other gifts that God offers him—Long life, wealth, fame—But through the avenue of Wisdom, he achieves all these things—and much more—including 700 wives.

In NGE Supreme Mathematics, we are taught that Wisdom is the 2—After the 1, which is Knowledge. It is the sure evidence of Knowledge—A reflection of Knowledge in action. And in my life—along my journey—all these understandings have proven themselves self-evident—Right and exact. Wisdom shows those in mental darkness the light. It manifests the path—the way. It is what we all need to live, to love, to grow, and to develop. The Sutras of the Buddha teach that without Wisdom, there is no gain. And I bear witness to the truth of that.

The sage Krishna once said—"You can study all day, pray all day, chant all day—but you will get to heaven faster if you hang with wise men."

Your net worth is your network—so to speak. The friend of a fool—is another fool. The friend of a wise man—is another wise man. A stupid person cannot help himself. So—choose your friends wisely. Drowning people sometimes kill their well-intentioned rescuers.

The Book of Proverbs says that King Solomon sought Wisdom—From the womb to the tomb, from the cradle to the grave—literally. That is another way of saying that he sought to reinvent himself all the time. That he sought rebirth. And just as one passes through the womb of a woman to become physically born in the flesh—One must also pass through the womb of Wisdom to achieve mental birth. And just like the bearing and birthing of a child—Wisdom often comes with pain.

Pain, joy, and fear have all manifested in me Wisdom. Which, like water, is an ever-flowing spring—A bottomless, endless source. A flow of life—That takes the shape of any vessel. That reveals itself in all bodies at all moments. For Wisdom is the way. Just as Allah is God—and God is Allah—Always has been. Always will be.

I will go into the 12 Jewels in a moment—But first, let me do my duty— And relay a truth. I want you to pin your eyes to the incredible power you alone possess. The only limits are the ones you place upon yourself. What lies dormant within you pales in comparison to what lies before you—or behind you. It is very simple:

G.O.D. = Good Orderly Direction. Living your truth is simple. Simplicity is the essence of all complexities. It is only as hard as you make it.

Understand this—and never be asleep: There are forces at work that will tirelessly try to destroy the Black male—Young and adult. To destroy the Black family unit. To destroy our backbones—our women. To destroy us in general. We are all a target for extinction—By this muthafuckin' demon. And we must do our duty—To protect, nurture, and educate the babies. Because they are the greatest. They are the future of our nation—Just as we once were.

There is a good book I read long ago—By Nathan McCall entitled "Makes Me Wanna Holler." In the book, he writes about the game of chess and how life itself is chess. And I agree. He writes:

"Mo' Battle taught me chess by explaining its philosophical parallels to life."

He said: "In life, the person who plots his course and thinks ahead before he acts—wins. It's the same with chess. One day, I made a move to capture a pawn and gave Mo' Battle an opening to take a valuable piece."

He smiled and said, "You can tell a lot about a person by the way he plays chess. People who think small in life tend to devote a lot of energy to capturing pawns—the least valuable piece on the board. They think they're playing to win—but they're not. But people who think big tend to go straight for the King or Queen—which wins you the game. The most important thing Mo' Battle taught me was that chess was a game of consequences."

He said, "Just as in life, there are consequences for every move you make in chess. Don't make a move without first weighing the potential consequences—because if you don't, you have no control over the outcome."

"I had never looked at life like that. I seldom weighed the consequences of anything—until after I had already done it. I'd do something crazy—and then brace myself for the consequences, whatever they happened to be. I had no control over the outcome. I had no control over my own life. When I thought about it—that was a hell of a way to live. Control outcomes. If I considered the consequences of moves before making them—that gave me a whole new way of looking at things."

In the 120-degree lessons, we learn that:

85% of the people are mentally deaf, dumb, and blind—To themselves and to who the True and Living God is. And they are slaves of mental death. We learn that the 10% know who the True and Living God is—But keep the masses asleep and medicated. They are the bloodsuckers of the poor. The fools that are evil incarnate—like Donald Trump.

The fools who began the war on drugs. The fools who began the war on Islam. And what you should know about the War on Drugs—And the War on Islam—Is that it is the war on you. A war on Black people. A war on all people of color worldwide. And it is not by coincidence. It is not by happenstance. It is by design.

The 10% perpetrate lies and conceal the truth by using mass media to bombard the people with propaganda.

They force you to accept things at face value—without investigating for yourself what is fact and what is false.

And we (NEG) are the 5%—the poor righteous teachers—who know the True and Living God and who are not slaves to mental death or poisonous influences.

We are the civilized ones, and it is our duty to teach the truth—to wake the dumb to their true selves—to resurrect the mentally dead. Dead to what is really going on in this world. You can Google the Nation of Gods and Earths and see what we are about. Our agenda has not changed since 1964—and I will continue to build strong in the world that Allah manifested.

I will continue striving—being a righteous man in my ways, words, and actions. A righteous God—born in His image, in His likeness. Doing the duty of a civilized person—not a savage in the pursuit of happiness. We are a strong-necked people—Easily led in the wrong direction—And hard to lead in the right direction. I say what has been said:

"Narrow is the straight gate, and wide is the road to ruin."

Love and respect yourself—first and foremost. God was not lying when He said in 1 Corinthians 3:16:

"The temple of God is in you."

You ain't got to go to church—All you got to do is look in the mirror. That image you see is a miracle of space dust—a living jewel—a perfect being. But when we embrace our base desires—and allow them to rule over us—We make gods out of our lower selves. That lower self makes a god out of getting high—out of chasing anything that moves—out of eating anything that tastes good. And these acts will take your life—not extend it. Strive to control yourself—to be Godly and civilized.

We are not unthinking beasts. The whole world follows trends set by the Black man and woman in America. If the Black man in the United States stood up and demanded change, the entire world would follow our lead. So, one of us must be a universal changer. One of us must make that choice to ride for our people. The one who will change this reality. Heed the call. As above, so below.

Get the knowledge of yourself. Understand your true and living self. The science of life is the science of YOU. There is innate greatness in man, the Original Man. And yes, we are the original people. The Sun does not kill us with its rays. We are the First and the Last. We were the first to settle and rule this planet, and we shall be the last to rule this planet. To remove the devil from this Earth and to bring peace from our efforts. We must break the mental chains of psychological slavery. Period.

Menticide is real. An everyday reality for our people. So is Willie Lynch Syndrome. Our people are so deeply affected by white supremacy that most don't even know that God is not a white boy with stringy hair in a picture.

This false image was given to us by those who know the power of imagery. The Black man is God, not a mystery spook. And the everyday reality for our young people is not knowing their true history. And therefore, they do not know their true selves. I put these words to paper to wake up my people, to return them mentally to their righteous selves.

I had to return to the essence of myself, as God of myself. I want to spark the seed of wisdom, a light in the minds of my people. To expand their sphere of thought, to open a new realm in their mentality. Knowing that we are the makers of ourselves. That it all begins and ends with us. We are the masters of our fate, the captains of our own ships.

Manifest your reality. Cultivate yourself. Or, you will be cultivated by something, or someone, that does not have your best interest at heart. Design your life or your life will be designed for you. Returning to the Jewels of Islam, now, I will relay to you our jewels, the jewels that help you shine—mentally, physically, and spiritually.

I was taught the meaning of fear at Shabazz's Fish & Chips all those years ago in Oak Park. Fear = False Emotions Appearing Real. Or False Expectations Appearing Real. Either way, it is not real. It is an illusion, like a fairy tale.

Emotions are Energy in Motion. They are either going up or down. You should control their direction. Not someone else. Not a circumstance. Not a situation. That is too much power to give anyone—or anything—over you. Fear, like doubt, is a self-imposed prison. It is a form of pollution. A poison. Do not partake.

The 12 Jewels of Islam

1. Knowledge

2. Wisdom

3. Understanding

4. Freedom

5. Justice

6. Equality

7. Food

8. Clothing

9. Shelter

10. Love

11. Peace

12. Happiness

Each jewel has its own unique meaning—And each jewel takes work and meditation to obtain and manifest in your life.

They break down like a chain reaction:

A man first attains Knowledge. That leads to Wisdom, which is the reflection of that Knowledge. Then, he attains Understanding. Which is the power to act on Wisdom.

With Understanding, he sees that he has Freedom. Because he has freed his mind from the ignorance that surrounds him. He has free will. But Freedom operates under the laws of Justice.

That equates to this reality: I am free to do anything. I can sell drugs, sleep with a woman out of lust, or even shoot a man who accidentally bumps into me without saying, "excuse me." But justice applies to every act we put into motion. Therefore, I must deal in equality because whether I like it or not, all men are created equal. By showing equality to each other, we activate freedom, justice, and equality—the 4th through 6th jewels, respectively. When internalized, these principles build an individual's character. Once you obtain them, you can then strive for food, clothing, and shelter—concepts that carry both mental and physical definitions.

Food nourishes the body, clothing protects it, and shelter provides a home. But mental food is the knowledge that nourishes the mind—wisdom, science, history, and our true story. Mental clothing is how you carry and present yourself—the way you move, walk, and articulate your thoughts. When you are covered in righteousness, even the most ragged clothes will carry dignity. Mental shelter is the protection of your mind, a bulletproof vest against the lies, corruption, and wickedness of this civilization.

When you possess these jewels, your residence—whether a cage or a small house in the ghetto—becomes a king's chamber. Mathematics formed my first governing code of ethics, but the jewels had the most profound effect on my attitude. When my world was crumbling, they reappeared in my mental landscape, where they had once lain dormant for years. I had learned these truths as a child in the hood. And even when my body was locked in hell, my mind was not. I had protection from these elements, and my thoughts were never shackled. I believed in myself, and that belief manifested in my life.

Most people let their bodies or circumstances control their minds. When someone is addicted to a drug like heroin, his body craves it—he physically needs it to function. Without it, he will experience unbearable sickness. But even though the body is enslaved by addiction, the mind is what disciplines you every time. When your psyche attains these jewels, it takes control. Even in physical hell, when you seek and embody the 12 jewels, your mind will lead your body, not the other way around. And once your mind leads, your body will follow—straight to heaven.

You don't obtain all 12 jewels at once. You must strive for them, meditate on their deeper meanings, and work to internalize them. But once you grasp the first nine, you are positioned to transform your life into something truly fulfilling. It's like obtaining love, which is the highest form of understanding—whether between two people or an all-encompassing love for humanity. Once you attain love, you then find peace. And finally, you arrive at happiness, which is total and complete satisfaction with yourself.

This means that nothing and no one else can make you happy—happiness must come from within. When you understand this, no one can rob you of it.

The final jewel applies to everyone on this planet—knowledge of self. This is the one kind of knowledge you cannot seek externally. You must allow it to happen through meditation, deep contemplation, and silence. You must separate yourself from the distractions of this world—TV, cell phones, the internet, and the constant noise designed to keep you mentally asleep. America is the great Satan, and you must protect your mind in a world designed to strip you of your natural self.

The rapper Nas (one of my favorite artists) has a song called "Black Zombie," which speaks to the reality of menticide—the deliberate destruction of a person's mind. Just as homicide is the killing of a human being, menticide is the killing of the mind. Many of our people suffer from this condition here in the wilderness of North America.

So, what is a zombie? A zombie is a corpse reactivated by secret means—walking, talking, living, and serving others—but still dead. The final stage of brainwashing is menticide. A dead mind is of no use to its owner because it is actually owned by the brainwashers. A brainwashed mind serves others but has no value to the self.

Kwabena F. Ashanti, in Psycho-Technology of Brainwashing, describes this condition. He explains that at least 85% of our people suffer tremendously from this trickery. They are walking dead, just like in the old-school horror movies. We must wake up from this slumber. The same brother above also revealed a disturbing reality:

New Africans (Black people) make up only 12.5 to 13% of the U.S. population, yet we account for nearly 50% of the arrests for murder. We make up almost 50% of the prison population. We make up 40% of those on death row. Yet, we consume only 15% of the drugs in this country, and still, we are arrested more than any other race for drug use.

Meanwhile, on the side enforcing the laws, there are almost no Black U.S. attorneys. This is not a coincidence. This is design.

Fewer than 5% of judges in America are Black, and the percentage of Black police officers is even lower. We are living in the new Jim Crow that Michelle Alexander spoke and wrote about so passionately in her book of the same name. That book is required reading for all of us who can see beyond the bullshit the media feeds us daily. This is why the system is so corrupt on every level—from law enforcement to the courts to the present government.

I implore you—never be self-conscious; be self-aware. The master scholar Albert Memmi, in his book Dominated Man: Notes Toward a Portrait, wrote:

"In every dominated man, there is a certain degree of self-rejection, born mostly of his downtrodden condition and exclusion… when the objective conditions are so weighty and corrosive, how could we imagine that they will not result in some destruction? That they will not warp the soul, the behavior, and even the very appearance of the oppressed man? The man who is conditioned not to like himself is bound to destroy himself."

Be aware of your condition. Set up your game plan with this in mind, and work your plan, period.

Many of us suffer from Post-Traumatic Slave Syndrome (PTSS), also known as Post-Traumatic Slave Disorder—a real diagnosis, look it up. We are also affected by Willie Lynch Syndrome—another real affliction, another real tool of oppression. Research it. And remember this—before you go to war with the devil over your people, make sure they actually want to be saved. Because some of them love being in chains.

Our people subliminally see God as white because of the false imagery of Christ that has been force-fed to us for generations. But the Black man is the original man—period.

The scholar Chashee McIntyre once explained our malady like this:

"The practice of imprisoning African American males has always been embedded in the structural design of this nation. From the very beginning, African Americans have lived (and still live) with the fear that if we do not end up in prison or in some other form of institution, someone in our families will. Our incarcerations do not occur because of criminality or accidents of injustice but because of the structural design of this nation. Institutionalization became the ultimate solution for how whites addressed the problem of having free Blacks in this country."

So, understand this—this is not happenstance. This is not a coincidence. This is not chance. And it damn sure isn't "manifest destiny." This was by design. This is by design.

And we need to be aware of that at all times. We must know the laws and understand the norms of this nation because, at the end of the day, this is still the same place that kidnapped us, stripped us of our names, our language, our culture, and forced us into labor to build its economy.

The blood of our forefathers built this nation, and these demons will die fighting to keep us from having equality. Throughout my seventeen years of captivity, it has been the love of my children, especially my baby girl Imara, that has sustained me through this crucible. Their love has strengthened me, inspired me, and kept me from losing myself completely.

The love of my family, those who refused to leave me for dead, carried me through the darkest times—while others did abandon me. My aunties, my sister Sharon my sister Felicia—they did their best considering the situation. When I was stuck in the SHU (solitary confinement) for two years in Tracy, fighting an assault case against a racist officer, I lost my old Earth—my mother. She passed away.

It was my niece Milly who called the prison to inform them that I had suffered a death in the family. When I was finally allowed a phone call, I had to stand inside a cage, like an animal, while some racist female counselor smugly asked me, "Do you want to see the chaplain?"

I told that cold-hearted b*tch, "Hell no." I explained to her racist ass that I had three kings who held me down—me, myself, and I. That's all I needed. I walked back to my cage with my head held high because I knew my mother was in a better place, reunited with our ancestors, no longer in pain, no longer suffering. If there is a heaven, she is in it.

I had already lost my sister Sharon while locked away in Pelican Bay State Prison. She, too, was now in a better place. Love has been the strongest force in my life—it has held me down all these years. But bitterness? Bitterness eats at you like a disease. And I could not afford that sickness. I could afford to be better. I could afford to master myself. I could afford to get smarter, stronger, and wiser. Oak Park took care of me for so many years. It's funny how, when I had no one, I still had the love of the P. That love kept my stomach full.

It was real ones like Big Virgel, Nigel, Nu, L.D., Ed Mallory, Terril, and my little sisters Black Barbie (Nicey), Big Blood, and Angelique who looked out for me. It was good women like Marjorie, who dropped a few dollars every time I needed it. It was brothers like Carl Murphy, Curty, Curtis Juniel, Billy D., Burger B., Lil Bliff, Mario Calhoun, and my nephew Lil G. It was Zo (Lorenzo Walsh) and too many others to list.

When I had nothing, when I was at my lowest, they put it in the hands of a woman who ran that play—so I could eat, so I could survive, so I could feed the ones around me who weren't as fortunate. And they did it out of love. From Pelican Bay to Folsom, I am nothing if not an Oak Park nigga. I have bled for my community, and when I needed them the most, they stood up for me. When my baby mama would have let me rot away and die in this hellhole, they stood up for the God. I remember Marjorie telling me, "Nigga, if you weren't fucking with that dirty-ass b*tch, you wouldn't be in jail." And how right she was. That b*tchwas Proverbs 5:3-5 personified. But love is the strongest force in the universe. Love is stronger than death. And next to love, the only force that compares is hate. It was the love I had for my kids, for my mother, and for myself that sustained me through the darkest times.

And to the women who risked their freedom for me—who ran the ball across enemy lines, who committed felony acts out of love—I salute you. It would ultimately be love that saved me from certain death.

The prophet Kahlil Gibran once wrote:

"It is my fervent hope that my whole life on this earth will forever be tears and laughter."

Wisdom, acquired through trial, error, and age, is fluid. It brings flexibility, adaptation, and liberation from the slavery of your past and your passions. Wisdom, grounded in supreme mathematics, has given me the ability to balance myself—to stand strong in the midst of chaos. I have fought every day of my life—and I will continue to strive forward. Because no matter what? I will never break my stride. No matter the circumstance or situation.

Then, out of the blue, this young lady reached out to me. I still had a few females looking out for me—some stragglers, half-heartedly getting at the God—but something about this woman hit me differently. I could feel it in my spirit—she was authentic.

At the time, I was being denied emails by the gatekeepers, those sadistic, racist devils running the prison system. I knew they were blocking my messages, so I wrote to the company that was sending my emails and requested copies. I sent them a self-addressed stamped envelope, asking them to send my messages back to me—because these crackers were blocking my blessings, just as they do at every turn.

The joint I was in would do anything to discourage mail and visitation. They thrived on foul, inhumane bullshit. But I am a psychopathic thinker, a planner, a plotter. So, eventually, I got my hands on that email—even though it had been sent five months earlier.

This was 2015. And this Queen—this woman—would be the one to give me my vision back. She re-rocked my mainframe. She sparked me back to mental full 20/20 vision. She bounced me back like cooked crack. She nourished my soul and returned my infinite power.

My thought process has always been infinite, never finite. I have always been in high pursuit of knowledge—and the more I know, the more I realize I don't know. That is the nature of true wisdom. Knowledge is infinite—it has no end. Everything in existence is built and maintained through knowledge. Me and Lil Mama are together to this day. A team of one. 1+2=3—the highest form of understanding, which is love.

There is a story in the Bible that I often reflect on—just as I do with the Holy Quran and the 120 Degrees—because I study all three. They enhance my spiritual knowledge, they center my humility, and they check my ego.

In this story, King Solomon uses wisdom to manifest love. When knowledge (1) and wisdom (2) are combined, love (3) is manifested. That is the basis of true understanding. Solomon, acting as an arbitrator, is asked to settle a dispute between two women—both claiming to be the mother of a child. To test them, he tells them he will cut the baby in half, giving each woman one equal half.

The woman, who is not the child's rightful mother, agrees immediately. But the real mother objects, crying out, "No! Let her keep the baby." She was willing to give up her child to save her child's life. This is true love.

When you acquire knowledge and wisdom, you will emphatically understand what love is. Not fake love. Not the superficial love you see every day. But true love—love that hopes all things, that is patient and kind, that endures all things. That other shit, that fair-weather love, will never stand up when times get hard.

A tremendous number of men do not understand women, just as a tremendous number of women do not understand men. One of the most misunderstood aspects of life is understanding each other. However, if you enter a relationship without knowledge and wisdom, one person will always dominate the other, and it will never be equal. That imbalance will always lead to negativity. There will be just-ice—but never justice.

The first step toward true understanding is introspection—looking at the man in the mirror. Men and women are not that different. The only thing that separates us is a tiny fraction of DNA.

The Honorable Elijah Muhammad taught that only 3% of DNA is missing in men—and that missing 3% resides in the woman. This ties into Genesis, where Allah removes man's rib to create the woman. Man is incomplete without woman.

There is only a 3% difference in our DNA—but that tiny chasm manifests as one of the most dynamic and powerful forces on Earth. If you are blessed to encounter and discover that missing piece of yourself in this life—what people call "the one"—then the synergy between you two is infinite. That is what put my rudder back on track. That is what righted my ship in these rough waters.

Love brought me back. Or rather, I brought myself back. I resurrected my dormant self—the part of me that had been buried deep within my core being. Losing someone so close to my heart, in the conditions I was in at the time, had literally broken my heart. Though I didn't realize it at the time.

One day, I went to the nurse line for a routine check-up. When she listened to my heart, she found an irregular heartbeat. I was rushed to the hospital—the same hospital where both my mother and father had passed away—right in the middle of Oak Park.

A few months later, I had to have my heart shocked back into regular sinus rhythm. The doctor told me I had Atrial Fibrillation (A-Fib). He concluded that I was too young to have developed this condition—especially since I was in otherwise perfect health.

I don't eat meat. I don't consume dairy. I eat like a gorilla—no dead flesh. So, it was determined that my A-Fib was stress-induced.

Yet, by the force of my will, I kept my mind calm and moved forward. Because life goes on—regardless of how we feel. This Earth keeps spinning at a terrific speed of 1,037 ⅓ mph. The cipher keeps rolling—like a rolling stone.

In the Hadith—a collection of the sayings of the Prophet Muhammad (PBUH)—there is a teaching that says the soul of Muhammad was the first soul created. From his soul, all other souls were brought into existence.

It is said that his soul enters the body of anyone who is mandated, called forth, or summoned—simply by existing. Like Jesus. Like Neo in The Matrix. Like Buddha, who is said to have had his soul out of play for thousands of years. This shows us that energy is eternal—it is always there, patiently waiting to manifest on this plane of existence.

We bring things into being through our will. Our pain. Our need. We manifest what we need into existence—to pull ourselves out of darkness. We reinvent ourselves through self-actualization. And as the Bible warns:

"Neither cast your pearls before swine, lest they trample them under their feet and turn and rend you."

Protect what is sacred to you. Not everyone deserves access to your divine resources—to your energy—to YOU. This is your world. Create what you will. Because in the end? It all begins and ends with YOU.

This is the heart sutra. The shortest sutra.
The body is nothing more than emptiness.
Emptiness is nothing more than body.
The body is exactly empty.
And emptiness is exactly body,
The other four aspects of human existence-feeling,
thought, will, and consciousness
Are likewise nothing more that emptiness,
and emptiness nothing more than they.
All things are empty.
Nothing is born, nothing dies,
nothing is pure, nothing is stained, nothing increases
And nothing decreases.
So, in emptiness, there is no body,
no feeling, no thought, no will, no consciousness.
There are no eyes, no ears, no nose, no tongue, no body, no mind
There is no seeing, no hearing, no smelling, no tasting, no touching, no
Imagining, there is nothing seen, nor heard, nor smelled nor tasted.
Nor touched, nor imagined. There is no ignorance, and no end to
ignorance. There is no old age and death there is no suffering,
no cause of suffering, no end

To suffering, no path to follow.
There is no attainment of wisdom and no wisdom
To attain.

OUTRO

To my children and extended family—this is for you. My sons, the TWINS Bryan and Brandon, the love is graveyard.

To my baby daughter, Imara Elon Sanders—whose name means strength and endurance in Kiswahili, and Elon, from the West African Hausa tribe, meaning God loves me—you were named with purpose. The Bible states that the best gift a parent can give their child is a name. A name that speaks power into their life. So every time your name is called, it will be calling forth strength and endurance all the days of your life.

To my oldest daughter and messy first princess, Jessica Alyssa Robinson, whom I love to the marrow of my bones. You are a phenomenal young warrior, Queen. I am very proud of your intellect and survival skills!! You can manifest any reality you see in your mind's eye as long as you stay focused.

Lastly, in the words of Og Mandino, the world's greatest salesman:

"I will greet this day with love in my heart, and how will I do this? Henceforth, I will look at things with love, and I will be born again. I will love the sun, for it warms my bones. Yet I will love the rain, for it cleanses my spirit. I will love the light, for it shows me the way. Yet I will love the darkness, for it shows me the stars. I will welcome happiness, for

110

it enlarges my heart. Yet I will endure sadness, for it opens my soul. I will acknowledge rewards, for they are my due. Yet I will welcome obstacles, for they are my challenge. There is no progress without struggle. Period."

Belief initiates and guides action—or it does nothing. To my Queen, on this chessboard of life—I love you. But even that word is not weighty enough to convey what I truly feel for you. So peace to my Earth.

To all my real ones resting in paradise—Beve Alston, Peg, Conrad, Bro. Jerome, Ponnie, Y.B., Shy, Marvin Keola, Shawn Collins, Gangsta Pete, Dinosaur, Tru Ru, Donald Willis Sr. and Jr., Chunk, Flashlight, Shawn Chaney. To everyone from the P. who lost their lives—naturally or otherwise—rest in power and peace. There are too many to name, but your names live on.

Shoutout to my day ones—Big Virgil, Jeff Baily, Stephen Miles, Dre Allen, Nigel Collins, Dupree Archie, Precious Archie, Linda Kay, The Crumps, The Blackwells, The Pitts, The Murphys, The Golstons, Lil Sister Chenequa, Black Nickey, Tyese, Big Blood, Lil Blue, Billy D., Burger B., Big Tony Allen, The Shavers, Black Ass Boo, Relly Darnell Smith, The Mad Pad, Main Main, Q.Q., The Hawkins, Leroy Woods, J, Hood, StunnaMan, Riko&Sweets The Parkers, The Miles, and the entire Oak Park community.

To the Oak Park Cipher of Black Souls, the lil homie Tear Drop, Bad Mouth—with his cheap ass, and everyone involved in this project— this is for you. And my next one will be even better. Last but never least—rest in power to:

Ora Marie Sanders, Sharon Yee, Uncles Big Floyd, Jimmy, JB, JT, Puddin, Johnny, Clarence, Ruben Sanders, Mama Lou, Paco, May, Janie, Granny—both Grannies, Mrs. Usher (Lena), Dante, and Marvin Draton.

To all the real ones—bulletproof love for life. I rest. Jerome Reed, Felicia Stanford. Rest easy, family......

The GOD M.S.

Peace! Shay Shay and Nini, I love you to death ......

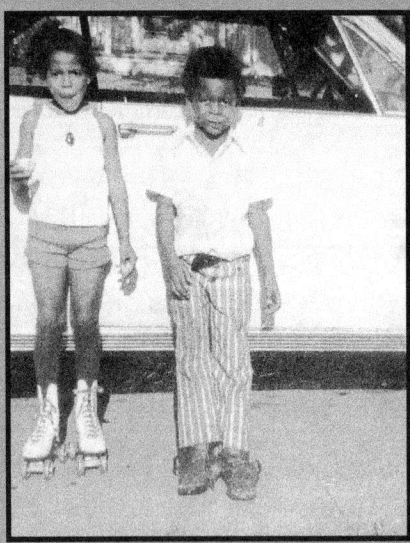

Golden Gate
MAY 8, 2024

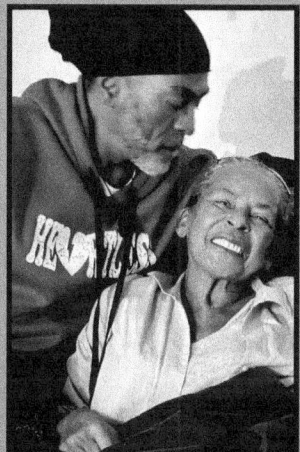

www.ingramcontent.com/pod-product-compliance
Lightning Source LLC
Chambersburg PA
CBHW071520120626
46550CB00006B/2296